Keynote
FOR BEGINNERS

Andrew Blake

TABLE OF CONTENTS

INTRODUCTION

Presentations don't need to look like documents pretending to be slides. Keynote doesn't open with a blank canvas—it opens with intent. Every element you add, align, animate, or rehearse is built to serve one thing: clarity. It's not about doing more, it's about making the moment feel lighter, sharper, and completely in sync with how you want to deliver it. You don't build slides in Keynote. You build momentum.

Every pixel feels anchored. Text knows where it belongs. Animations don't distract—they follow logic. You can step through a pitch, prototype an interface, or present a class report, all without leaving the flow of what you're trying to say. Shapes scale perfectly. Transitions don't stutter. Fonts look like they were chosen instead of defaulted. You can feel when a slide is finished, not because you've run out of space, but because it already works.

Keynote on Mac is powerful. On iPad, it's tactile. On iPhone, it's nimble. But no matter where you're working, you can collaborate, edit, review, and rehearse in real time. Whether you're presenting live, streaming remotely, or handing off the final file, the polish stays. The delivery feels intentional. And the silence between slides starts feeling like design, not hesitation.

WHAT IS KEYNOTE? OVERVIEW AND FEATURES

Keynote is Apple's presentation software, part of the iWork suite, designed to help users create visually engaging and dynamic presentations. Introduced in 2003, Keynote was initially developed for internal use by Apple executives, including Steve Jobs, to deliver keynote addresses at events.

1

Recognizing its potential, Apple released Keynote to the public, offering users a tool that combines ease of use with powerful features.

Over the years, Keynote has evolved significantly, incorporating advanced functionalities such as real-time collaboration, interactive charts, and cinematic transitions. Its integration across macOS, iOS, and iPadOS ensures a seamless experience, allowing users to create, edit, and present from any Apple device. With regular updates, Keynote continues to enhance its capabilities, aligning with the latest technological advancements and user needs.

Keynote's intuitive interface and robust feature set make it suitable for a wide range of users, from students crafting class presentations to professionals delivering business pitches. Its emphasis on design and functionality enables users to convey their ideas effectively, making Keynote a preferred choice for creating compelling presentations.

DYNAMIC THEMES AND TEMPLATES

Keynote offers a variety of professionally designed themes and templates, providing users with a solid foundation for their presentations. These themes ensure consistency in design elements such as fonts, colors, and layouts, allowing users to focus on content creation. Customization options enable users to tailor these templates to suit specific needs, ensuring each presentation aligns with its intended purpose.

CINEMATIC TRANSITIONS AND ANIMATIONS

Keynote includes a range of cinematic transitions and animations, such as Magic Move, which allows for smooth object transitions between slides. These features add a dynamic element to presentations, enhancing audience engagement. Users can animate text, images, and shapes, controlling the timing and sequence to create a polished and professional delivery.

REAL-TIME COLLABORATION
With iCloud integration, Keynote facilitates real-time collaboration, enabling multiple users to work on a presentation simultaneously. Changes are synced across devices, and collaborators can see edits as they happen. This feature streamlines the collaborative process, making it easier for teams to develop and refine presentations together.

INTERACTIVE CHARTS AND DATA VISUALIZATION
Keynote provides tools for creating interactive charts and data visualizations, allowing users to present complex information clearly and effectively. Users can choose from various chart types, including bar, line, and pie charts, and customize them to match the presentation's design. Interactive elements enable audiences to engage with the data, fostering a deeper understanding of the content.

INTEGRATION WITH APPLE DEVICES
Keynote seamlessly integrates with other Apple devices and services, enhancing its functionality. Users can control presentations using their iPhone or Apple Watch, providing flexibility during delivery. Additionally, Keynote supports Apple Pencil on iPad, enabling users to draw and annotate slides directly, adding a personal touch to their presentations.

ACCESSIBILITY FEATURES
Keynote includes a range of accessibility features to accommodate diverse user needs. These features include VoiceOver support, closed captioning, and keyboard navigation, ensuring that presentations are accessible to all audiences. By prioritizing inclusivity, Keynote enables users to create presentations that can be effectively delivered and understood by everyone.

Keynote combines intuitive design with powerful features, providing users with the tools needed to create engaging and effective presentations. Its seamless integration across Apple devices, coupled with regular updates and enhancements, ensures that Keynote remains a leading choice for presentation software.

KEYNOTE VS. POWERPOINT: WHICH ONE TO USE?

There's a moment between opening a slide deck and presenting it—where the tool you choose either gets out of the way or fills the screen with options. That moment feels different in Keynote than it does in PowerPoint. Keynote gives you layout, rhythm, animation, and clarity without asking too many questions first. PowerPoint gives you structure, menus, and deep tools that work across industries and file types, no matter the operating system.

You can create a polished presentation in either. You can share it, animate it, export it, present it live. But the way you get there—and the way it feels while you're doing it—depends on the app you're using.

PLATFORM COMPATIBILITY

Keynote is exclusive to Apple's ecosystem, available on macOS, iOS, and iPadOS devices. It also offers a web-based version through iCloud, allowing limited access on non-Apple devices. This tight integration ensures a consistent experience across Apple hardware but may pose challenges when collaborating with users on other platforms.

PowerPoint, on the other hand, boasts extensive cross-platform support.It's available on Windows, macOS, iOS, Android, and through web browsers via Microsoft 365. This broad compatibility facilitates collaboration and accessibility, especially in diverse organizational environments.

USER INTERFACE AND EASE OF USE

Keynote offers a minimalist and user-friendly interface, emphasizing simplicity and ease of navigation. Its design-centric approach allows users to focus on content creation without being overwhelmed by numerous toolbars or options. This streamlined interface is particularly appealing to users who prioritize aesthetics and straightforward functionality.

PowerPoint features a more complex interface with a ribbon-style toolbar that categorizes tools into various tabs. While this provides quick access to a wide array of features, it may present a steeper learning curve for new users. However, for those familiar with Microsoft's suite of applications, the interface offers a sense of familiarity and consistency.

DESIGN AND TEMPLATES

Keynote is renowned for its high-quality templates and design elements. It offers a selection of elegant themes and smooth animations, enabling users to create visually appealing presentations with minimal effort. The emphasis on design aesthetics makes Keynote a preferred choice for creative professionals and those seeking polished visuals.

PowerPoint provides a vast library of templates and design tools, catering to a wide range of presentation needs. Its "Design Ideas" feature offers AI-powered suggestions to enhance slide layouts, aiding users in creating professional-looking presentations. While some default templates may appear dated, the extensive customization options allow for tailored designs.

COLLABORATION AND SHARING

Keynote integrates with iCloud to support real-time collaboration among Apple users. Users can share presentations via links, allowing others to view or edit documents simultaneously. However, collaboration with non-Apple users may be limited due to platform restrictions.

PowerPoint excels in collaborative features, especially within the Microsoft 365 ecosystem. It supports real-time co-authoring, version history, and seamless integration with Microsoft Teams and OneDrive. This robust collaboration framework is advantageous for teams operating across different platforms.

ADVANCED FEATURES AND FUNCTIONALITY

Keynote offers a range of features focused on delivering visually engaging presentations, such as cinematic transitions, interactive charts, and support for Apple Pencil on iPad. While it covers essential presentation needs, it may lack some advanced functionalities required for complex data analysis or automation.

PowerPoint provides a comprehensive set of advanced features, including extensive charting tools, macros, and integration with other Microsoft Office applications. Its versatility makes it suitable for detailed data presentations, automation tasks, and integration into broader workflows.

COST AND ACCESSIBILITY

Keynote is free to download and use on Apple devices, making it an accessible option for users within the Apple ecosystem. Its cost-effectiveness is appealing to individuals and organizations already invested in Apple hardware.

PowerPoint typically requires a subscription to Microsoft 365 or a one-time purchase, which may be a consideration for budget-conscious users. However, its widespread use and feature-rich environment often justify the investment for many professionals and businesses.

WHICH ONE TO USE?

The choice between Keynote and PowerPoint hinges on your specific needs and operating environment. If you're deeply integrated into the Apple ecosystem and prioritize design aesthetics and ease of use, Keynote is a compelling choice.Its seamless integration with Apple devices and user-friendly interface make it ideal for creating visually appealing presentations with minimal effort.

Conversely, if you require advanced features, extensive collaboration tools, and cross-platform compatibility, PowerPoint stands out as the more versatile option. Its robust functionality and widespread adoption in professional settings make it a reliable choice for complex presentation needs.

Both Keynote and PowerPoint are powerful tools capable of delivering effective presentations. Your decision should align with your workflow preferences, collaboration requirements, and the platforms you and your audience utilize.

NAVIGATING THE KEYNOTE INTERFACE

- **Keynote Interface (macOs)**

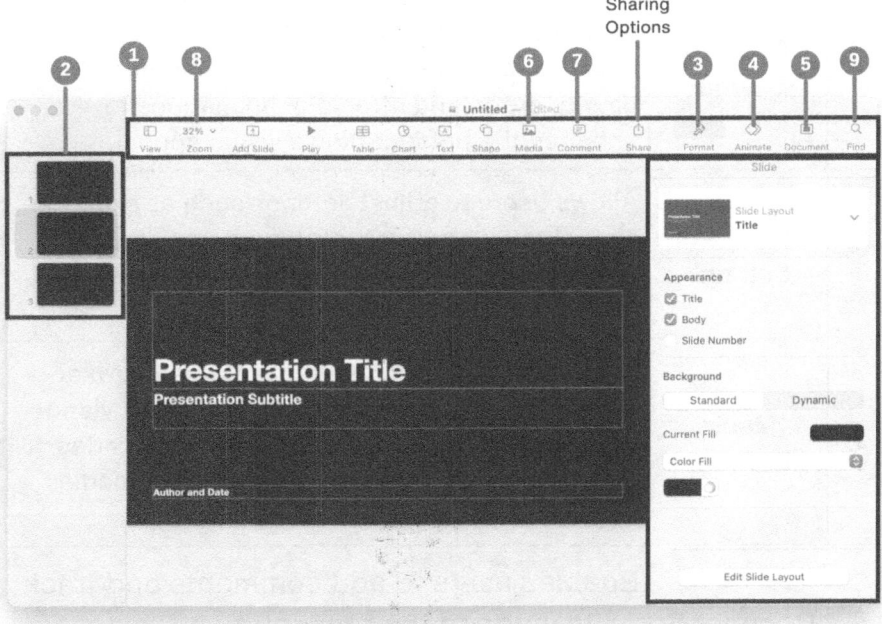

	Interface Element	Description
1	Toolbar	Provides quick access to commonly used actions such as adding slides, tables, charts, text boxes, shapes, and media. It also includes buttons for formatting, collaborating, and playing the presentation.
2	Slide Navigator	Allows users to quickly navigate between slides, reorder them, or group them into sections for better organization.

3	**Format Sidebar**	Offers contextual formatting options, including style, layout, and arrangement settings, allowing users to fine-tune the appearance and positioning of elements within the presentation.
4	**Animate Sidebar**	When an object is selected, the Animate sidebar provides options to add build-in, action, and build-out animations. Users can customize the timing, order, and effects of animations to enhance the presentation's visual appeal.
5	**Document Settings**	Allows users to adjust settings such as slide size, aspect ratio, and presentation theme. It also provides options to add presenter notes and set up the presentation for collaboration.
6	**Media Browser**	Accessible via the toolbar, the Media Browser allows users to insert images, audio, and video from their Photos, Music, and Movies libraries. It streamlines the process of adding multimedia content to presentations.
7	**Comments and Track Changes**	Enables users to add comments and track edits made to the presentation. This feature is essential for collaborative work, allowing contributors to provide feedback and review changes efficiently.
8	**Zoom Controls**	Located at the bottom right corner, these controls allow users to adjust the zoom level of the presentation for better visibility and navigation.
9	**Search Field**	Positioned in the toolbar, the search field enables users to quickly find specific text within the presentation, facilitating efficient editing and review.

- **Keynote Interface (iOS)**

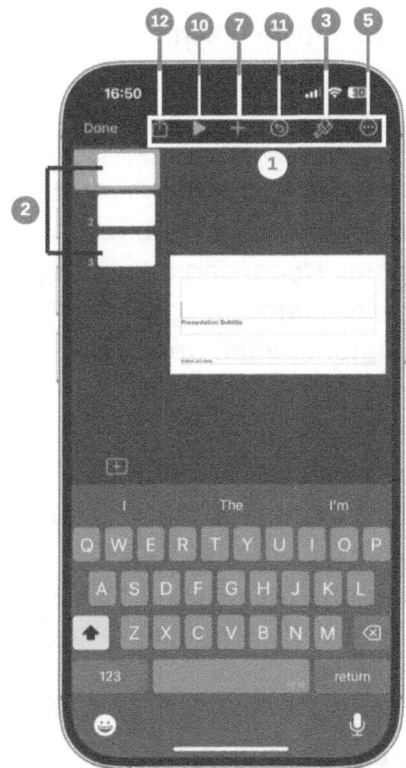

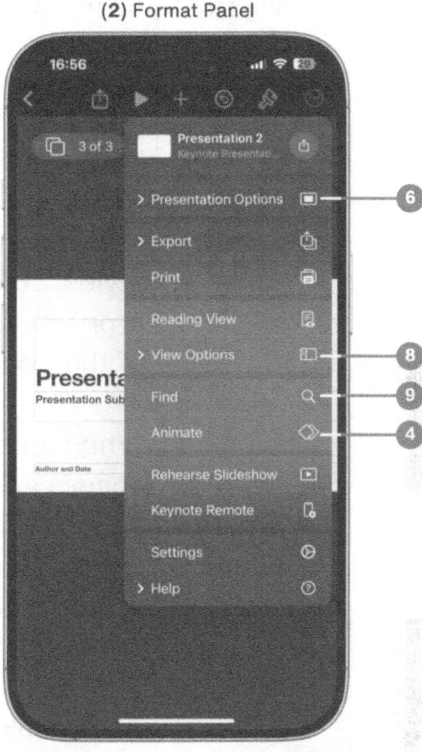

(2) Format Panel

	INTERFACE ELEMENT	DESCRIPTION
1	Toolbar	Positioned at the top of the screen, the toolbar provides access to essential functions such as adding slides, tables, charts, text boxes, shapes, and media. It also includes options for formatting, collaborating, and playing the presentation. The toolbar adapts based on the selected object, offering relevant tools for the task at hand.

2	**Slide Navigator**	Accessible by tapping the slide navigator icon, this feature displays thumbnails of all slides in the presentation, allowing users to navigate between slides and manage the presentation structure efficiently.
3	**Format Panel**	When an object is selected, the Format Panel appears, presenting contextual formatting options. Users can adjust text styles, colors, alignment, and other properties to customize the appearance of their content.
4	**Animate Options**	When an object is selected, users can access animation options to add build-in, action, and build-out effects. These animations enhance the presentation's visual dynamics and can be customized for timing and order.
5	**Document Settings**	Accessible via the More button, this section allows users to adjust settings such as slide size, aspect ratio, and presentation theme. It also provides options to add presenter notes and set up the presentation for collaboration.
6	**Presenter Display**	When presenting, Keynote offers a presenter display that shows the current slide, next slide, presenter notes, and a timer. This feature helps presenters stay organized and maintain a smooth flow during the presentation.

7	**Media Insertion**	Through the Insert Menu, users can access their Photos library to insert images directly into the presentation, facilitating the inclusion of visual content.
8	**Zoom and View Options**	Pinch-to-zoom gestures allow users to adjust the presentation's zoom level. Additionally, view options enable users to switch between different presentation views for optimal editing and reading experiences.
9	**Search Function**	Accessible via the magnifying glass icon, the search function enables users to locate specific text within the presentation quickly, streamlining the editing process.
10	**Play Button**	The Play button begins the presentation from the current slide or the beginning, enabling full-screen playback with presenter tools. Ideal for previewing or delivering a live presentation.
11	**Undo Button**	Tapping the Undo button reverses the most recent change. Essential for quickly correcting mistakes without disrupting workflow.
12	**Share Button**	The Share button allows users to export or collaborate on the presentation. Users can share via iCloud, AirDrop, or other apps, and manage permissions such as view-only or edit access.

CHAPTER 1

Creating and Structuring Presentations

A presentation doesn't begin on the first slide—it begins the moment you open a blank canvas. Before anything is said, the space starts shaping what will be heard. Every new theme sets a tone. Every layout defines the flow. What begins as structure quickly becomes rhythm, and that rhythm is what the audience will follow from the first word to the last transition.

Keynote is designed to remove friction from that process. It gives you choices without chaos. Clean templates. Purposeful layouts. Just the right balance between structure and control. Whether you're preparing three slides or thirty, the process stays focused and uninterrupted. It's less about building a slideshow and more about setting the stage. You adjust, refine, move things around—but the structure stays balanced. Every slide knows its place. Every element falls in line. And when it's time to present, the result feels cohesive from the first frame to the final screen. Because the work wasn't just designed to say something—it was built to carry something forward, clearly and confidently.

STARTING A NEW PRESENTATION

Every presentation begins with a blank canvas. In Keynote, that canvas is more than just empty space—it's a starting point designed for clarity and creativity. From the moment you open the app, the tools are there to help you shape your ideas into a compelling narrative. Themes, layouts, and intuitive controls guide you seamlessly from concept to creation.

Starting a new presentation isn't about filling slides with content; it's about structuring your message with intention. Keynote provides a streamlined environment where each choice—from selecting a theme to arranging slides—supports your storytelling. With thoughtful design and responsive features, your ideas take center stage, ready to engage and inform.

Launching Keynote and Creating a New Presentation

Opening Keynote presents you with a range of themes to kickstart your presentation. These themes offer pre-designed layouts that can be customized to fit your content.

1. Open the **Keynote** app on your Mac.

2. If the theme chooser doesn't appear, select **File** > **New** from the menu bar.

3. Browse through the available themes and double-click one to select it.

Once a theme is selected, a new presentation window opens, ready for you to add content.

Adding and Managing Slides

Building your presentation involves adding slides and organizing them effectively. Keynote provides various slide layouts to accommodate different types of content.

To add a new slide:

1. Click the **Add Slide** button in the toolbar.

2. Choose a layout from the dropdown menu that suits your content.

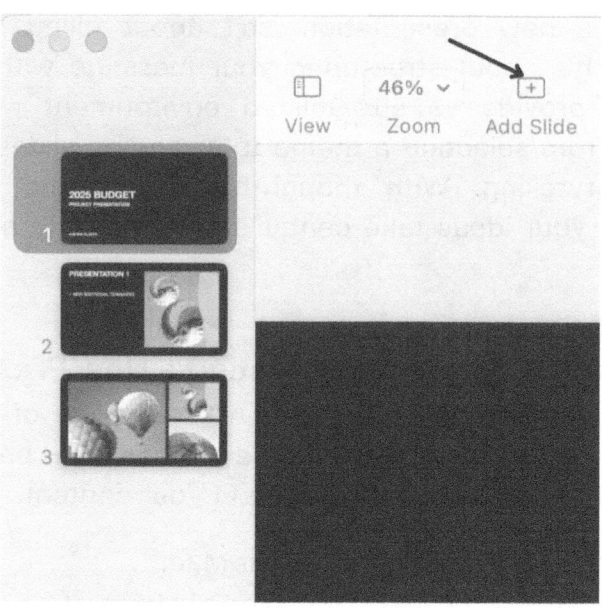

To rearrange slides:

1. Drag and drop slides in the slide navigator on the left side of the window.

This flexibility allows you to structure your presentation logically and coherently.

Saving and Naming Your Presentation

Keynote automatically saves your work, but assigning a clear name and location helps with organization.

1. Choose **File** > **Save** from the menu bar.

2. Enter a name for your presentation.

3. Select a location on your **Mac** or **iCloud Drive**.

4. Click **Save**.

Storing your presentation in iCloud allows for easy access across your Apple devices.

Adjusting Slide Size and Aspect Ratio

Tailoring the slide size ensures your presentation displays correctly on various screens.

1 Click the **Document** button in the toolbar.

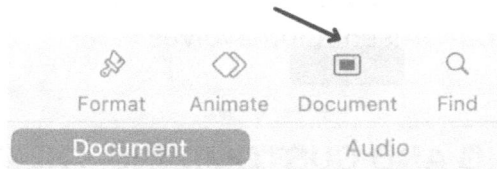

2 In the **Document** tab, click the Slide Size dropdown menu.

3 Choose a preset size or select **Custom Slide Size** to enter specific dimensions.

Adjusting the aspect ratio helps maintain visual consistency across different display formats.

Auto-Save and Version Control

Keynote's auto-save feature ensures your work is always up to date. You can also access previous versions of a presentation if you need to recover changes or review earlier drafts.

To view versions:

1 Choose **File > Revert To > Browse All Versions**.

2 Use the timeline on the right to scroll through saved versions.

3 Click **Restore** to revert to an earlier version if needed.

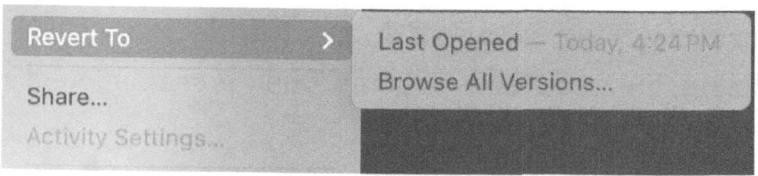

This built-in version control adds a layer of protection and flexibility as your presentation evolves.

CHOOSING AND CUSTOMIZING THEMES

Every presentation begins with a theme.In Keynote, themes provide a cohesive set of layouts, fonts, and colors that set the tone for your content.They offer a foundation that balances design and functionality, allowing you to focus on your message.

Customizing themes enables you to align your presentation with your brand or personal style. Whether you're adjusting colors, fonts, or slide layouts, Keynote offers intuitive tools to make these changes seamless. By tailoring themes to your needs, you ensure consistency and professionalism throughout your presentation.

Selecting a Theme

Keynote offers a variety of pre-designed themes to suit different presentation styles. Choosing the right theme provides a consistent look and feel across your slides.

1. Open Keynote and choose **File > New**.

2. Browse the theme chooser and double-click a theme to start your presentation.

Themes include coordinated fonts, colors, and layouts, providing a polished starting point for your content.

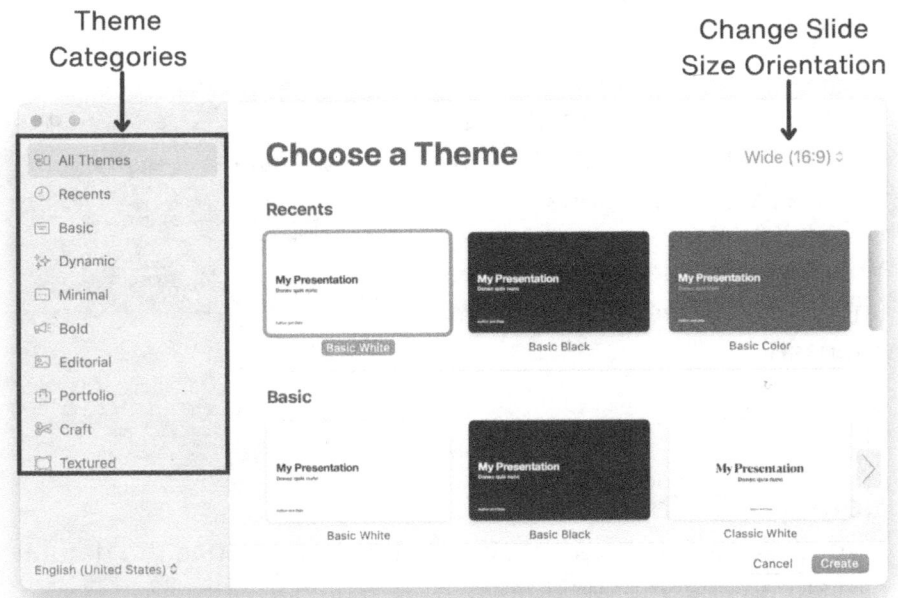

Theme Categories

Change Slide Size Orientation

Changing the Theme of an Existing Presentation

You can change the theme of your presentation at any time without losing your content. This allows you to update the design to better match your message.

1. Open your presentation in Keynote.

2. Choose **File** > **Change Theme**.

3. Select a new theme from the chooser and click **Choose**.

If you've made customizations to your slides, you can choose to retain or override them when applying the new theme.

Creating a Custom Theme

After customizing your slide layouts, you can save them as a new theme for future use. This is useful for maintaining branding consistency across multiple presentations.

1. With your presentation open, choose **File** > **Save Theme**.

2. Enter a name for your theme and choose where to save it.

Click **Add to Theme Chooser** ❸ to make it available for future presentations.

Your custom theme will appear under **My Themes** in the theme chooser.

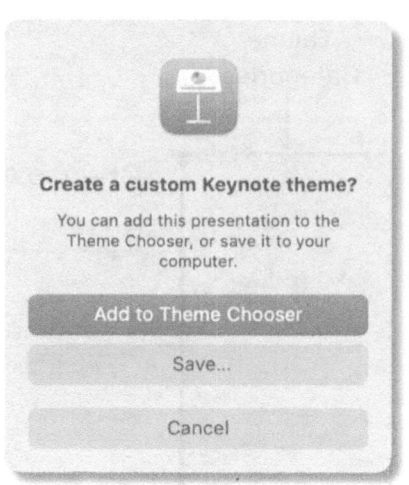

Setting a Default Theme

If you frequently use a specific theme, setting it as the default can streamline your workflow.

❶ Open Keynote and choose **Keynote** > **Settings**.

❷ In the **General tab**, select **Use** theme.

❸ Click **Change Theme**, select your preferred theme, and click **Choose**.

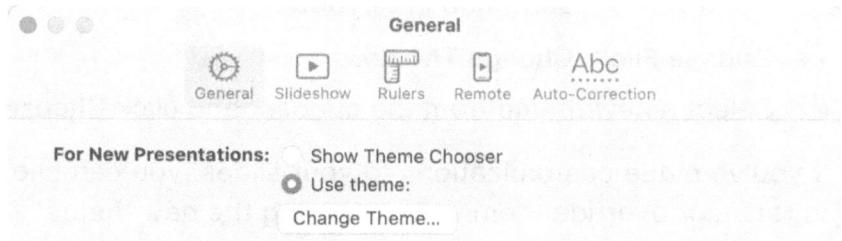

New presentations will now automatically use your selected default theme.

MANAGING SLIDES AND LAYOUTS

A presentation is more than a sequence of slides; it's a structured narrative. In Keynote, managing slides and layouts is about orchestrating this narrative with clarity and precision. Each slide serves a purpose, and the layout determines how content is presented and perceived.

Keynote offers intuitive tools to add, organize, and customize slides, ensuring your message flows seamlessly. By mastering slide management and layout customization, you can create presentations that are both visually cohesive and impactful.

Reordering Slides

The sequence of slides influences the narrative flow. Keynote allows you to rearrange slides effortlessly.

1 In the slide navigator, click and drag a slide to a new position.

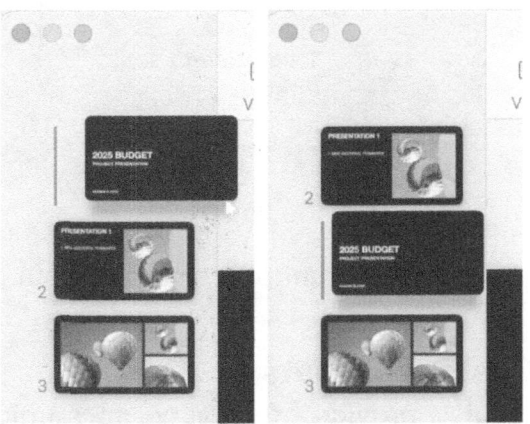

2 Release the mouse button to place the slide.

This flexibility helps maintain logical progression in your presentation.

Grouping Slides

Organizing slides into groups can simplify complex presentations.

1 Select multiple slides in the navigator.

2 Control-click and choose **Group Slides**.

Grouped slides can be collapsed or expanded, aiding in navigation and editing.

Applying Slide Layouts

Consistent layouts enhance visual coherence.

1 Select a slide.

2 In the **Format** sidebar, click **Slide Layout**.

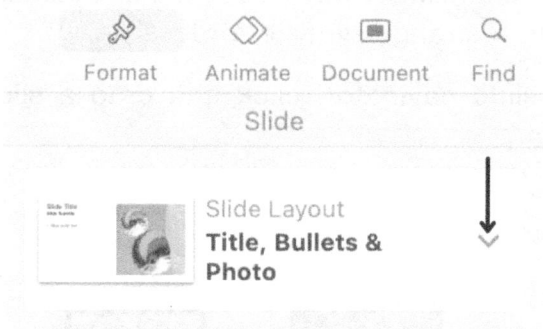

3 Choose a layout from the list.

Applying layouts ensures uniformity across your presentation.

Creating Custom Layouts

Custom layouts provide flexibility for unique content structures.

1 In E**dit Slide Layouts**, click the **Add Layout button**.

2 Design the layout by adding placeholders and design elements.

③ Name the layout for easy identification. Click **Done** to finalize.

Custom layouts can be reused across multiple presentations.

Deleting Slides

Removing unnecessary slides streamlines your presentation.

① Select the slide in the navigator.

② Press **Delete** or choose **Edit > Delete**.

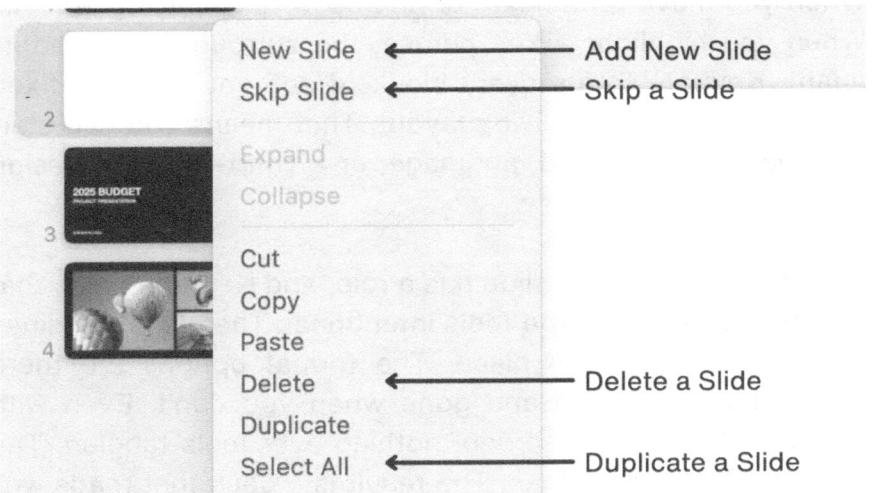

Duplicating Slides

Duplicating slides saves time when creating similar content.

① Select the slide.

② Choose **Edit > Duplicate**. Or   Control-click and choose **Duplicate**

The duplicated slide retains all elements of the original.

CHAPTER 2

Adding and Formatting Content

A presentation becomes real the moment content starts to take shape on the slide. Not just text, but the way it's placed, how it's styled, and how it interacts with everything around it. The process is simple, but not static—every object responds. When you move text closer to an image, the spacing adjusts. When you highlight a key phrase, the surrounding elements adapt. Keynote treats every block of content not as a fixed item, but as part of a living layout. That means you can start anywhere—with a word, an image, or a chart—and the design keeps up.

Everything added to a slide has a role, and Keynote helps that role stay clear. The type feels intentional. The alignment lines keep the structure in place. The format options are there when you need them and gone when you don't. Even with multiple elements on screen, nothing ever feels tangled. The editing space stays clean. The result is a deck that reads well before it's even presented—and feels balanced from the first slide to the last.

INSERTING AND EDITING TEXT

A presentation begins with words. The layout supports the message, but it's the text that drives it. Whether it's a headline introducing your topic or a note beneath a chart, every word on a slide contributes to the story you're telling. Keynote makes working with text straightforward, allowing you to focus on the message rather than the tool.

We'll use a single slide as our working example: a title slide for a presentation called "**2025 Product Strategy**". We'll insert the title, add a subtitle, and refine each part using Keynote's formatting tools. Each step builds upon the previous one, guiding you from a blank layout to a clean, styled slide.

Adding a Title and Subtitle

The title slide typically includes two text fields: one for the main title and another for supporting context. We'll enter both.

1 Open a new presentation and select the Title & Subtitle layout from the slide chooser.

2 Click the placeholder text that says "Title", then type: **2025 Product Strategy**.

3 Click the "Subtitle" field, then type: **Quarterly Objectives & Key Metrics**.

Now you have a basic title slide set up and ready for formatting.

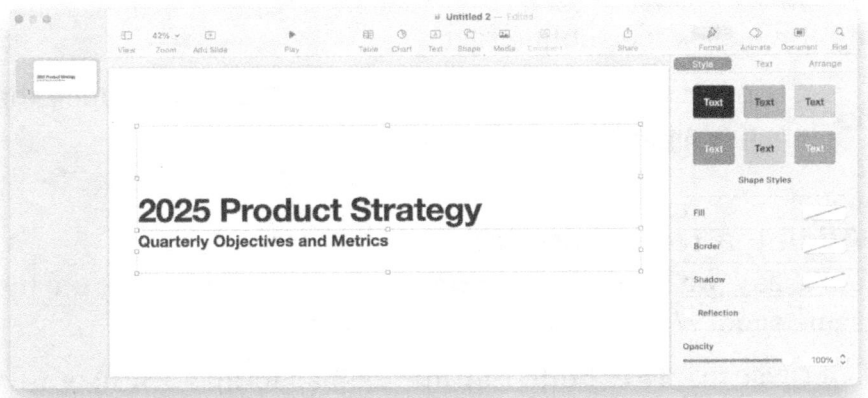

Formatting Text (Bold, Italics, Size)

Next, we'll style the title to make it more prominent and give the subtitle a more subtle tone.

1 Click on the title text to select it.

2 In the **Format** sidebar, under the **Text** tab, set the font to **Helvetica Neue Bold**, size **120 pt**.

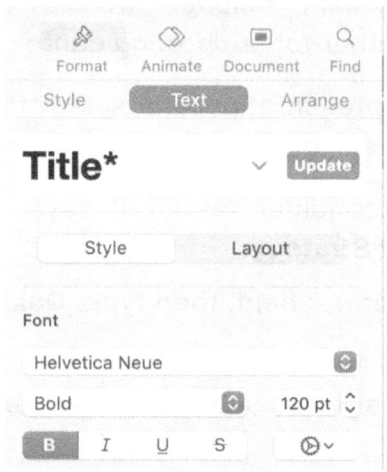

3 Center the text horizontally using the alignment buttons.

4 Now click the subtitle text.

5 Change the font style to Italic, size **55 pt**, and reduce the opacity slightly (to 80%) for a lighter touch.

Adding a Third Text Box

Let's say we want to include the presenter's name on the same slide. We'll add a custom text box.

1 Click the **Text** button in the toolbar to insert a new text box

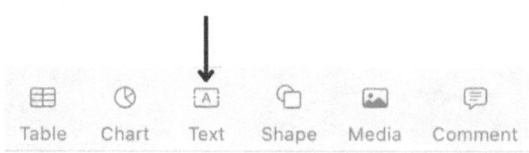

2   Drag it to the lower-right corner of the slide.

3   Type: **Presented by Jordan Kim**.

4   Use the same font used before, size 36 pt, and align it right.

Adjusting Text Color and Background Fill

To give the title more distinction, we'll add a color and background fill.

1   Select the title text box.

2   In the Format sidebar, under **Style**, click the **Fill** dropdown and choose **Color Fill**.

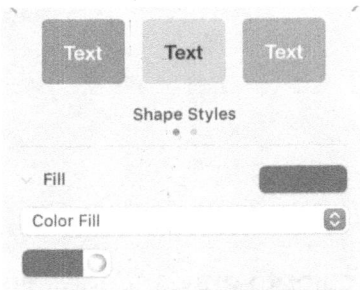

3   Select a **bold blue tone** (or a custom brand color).

4   Under **Text Color**, switch the text to **White** for contrast.

This styling makes the title pop without overwhelming the slide.

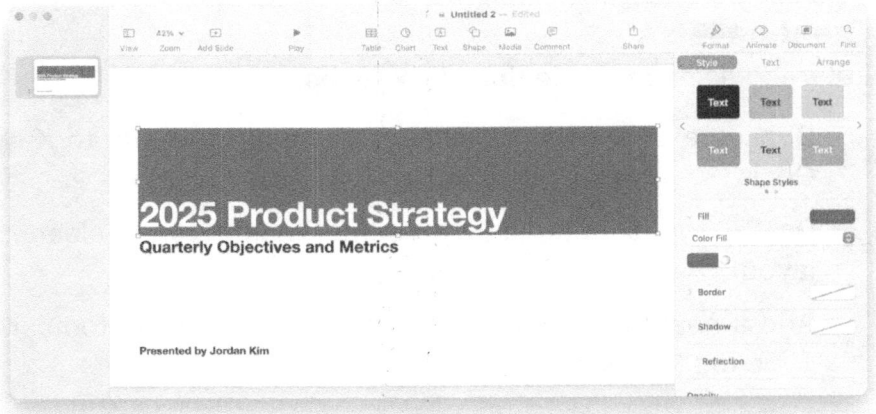

Adding Borders and Shadows

Now we'll give the subtitle a subtle shadow and border for depth.

1 Select the subtitle text box.

2 In the **Style** section, click **Border** and choose **Line**.

3 Set the border color to gray and the thickness to **1 pt**.

4 Then, enable **Shadow**, set blur to **2 pt**, and adjust opacity to **50%**.

Now we'll give the subtitle a subtle shadow and border for depth.

Creating Lists

Let's add a second slide titled **Key Goals**.

1 Duplicate your existing slide and change the title to **Key Goals**.

2 Delete the subtitle and presenter name for a cleaner layout.

3 Add a new text box using the Text button in the toolbar. Type the following text:

Expand into three new markets
Improve product retention by 20%
Launch Q3 software updates
Streamline onboarding workflow

4 Select all text.

5 In the **Format** sidebar, under the **Text** tab, locate the **Bullets & Lists** section.

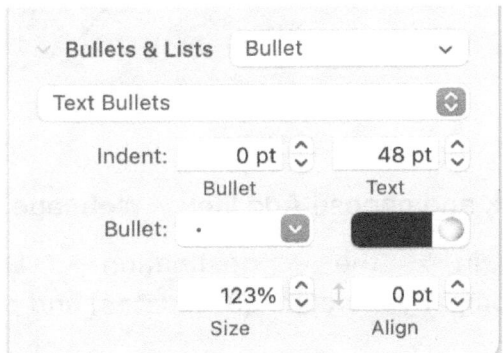

6 Choose **Bullet** style. Then, click **Bullet Options** to customize the appearance—change the bullet to a checkmark or colored dot, adjust indent spacing, and align to your brand.

This creates a simple, clean list that fits our product strategy theme and continues our formatting structure.

Applying Hyperlinks to Text

Now we'll add a hyperlink to one of the list items for additional context—say, linking "Q3 software updates" to a webpage.

1 Highlight Launch Q3 software updates in the bullet list.

Key Goals

- Expand into three new markets
- Improve product retention by 20%
- Launch Q3 software update
- Streamline onboarding worl

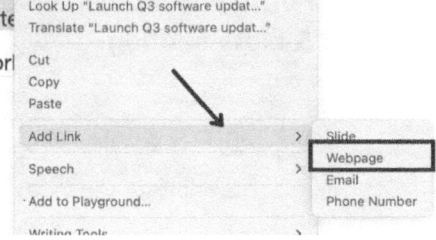

2 Right-click and choose **Add Link** > **Webpage**.

3 Paste in the destination URL (e.g., **https://companysite.com/q3-updates**) and press **Return**.

The text remains part of the list, but is now clickable—perfect for interactive or shared presentations.

Locking and Unlocking Text Boxes

Once your titles, lists, and label elements are finalized, locking them can prevent accidental shifts while working on other elements.

1 Select the **Key Goals** title text box.

2 Go to the **Arrange** tab in the Format sidebar.

3 Scroll down and click **Lock**.

To make changes later, select the locked object and choose Unlock from the same **Arrange** menu.

WORKING WITH IMAGES, SHAPES, AND ICONS

Visual elements transform a presentation from informative to impactful. Images, shapes, and icons not only enhance aesthetic appeal but also aid in conveying complex information succinctly. Keynote offers intuitive tools to seamlessly integrate these elements, allowing for a harmonious blend of text and visuals.

Continuing with our **"2025 Product Strategy"** presentation, we'll enrich our slides by incorporating relevant images, designing custom shapes, and utilizing icons to represent key concepts. Each step will build upon the previous, ensuring a cohesive and visually engaging presentation.

Adding and Positioning Images

Copy the second slide and change the title to "Market Overview" To illustrate our market expansion plans, we'll add a relevant image to the "Market Overview" slide.

1. Navigate to the **"Market Overview"** slide.

2. Click on the **Media** button in the toolbar and select **Choose**.

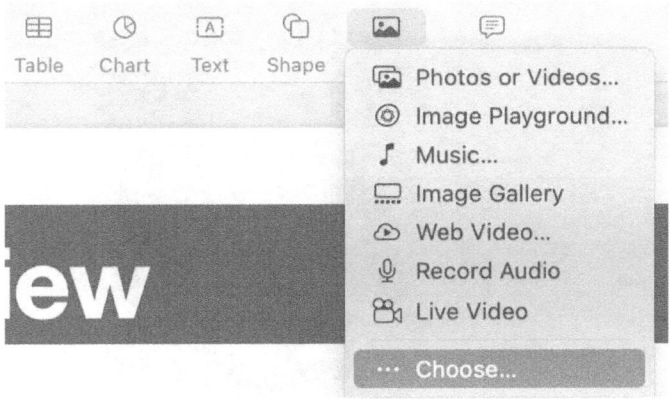

3 Locate and select an image depicting global markets or relevant imagery.

4 Click **Insert** to add the image to the slide.

5 Resize and position the image to complement the existing text without overshadowing it.

This visual addition reinforces the slide's message, providing a graphical representation of the content.

Masking and Cropping Images

To focus on specific regions in the image, we'll use Keynote's masking feature.

1 Select the inserted image.

2 Click on the Image tab in the **Format** sidebar.

3 Click **Edit Mask**.

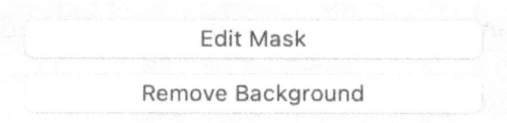

4 Adjust the mask to highlight the desired area.

5 Click **Done** to apply the mask.

Manually Crop Image

Utilizing Background Removal

To remove unwanted backgrounds from images, we'll use the **Remove Background** tool.

① Select the image with the background to remove.

② Click on the **Image** tab in the **Format** sidebar.

③ Click **Remove Background**.

④ Click and drag over the background area to make it transparent.

⑤ Release the mouse button and click **Done**.

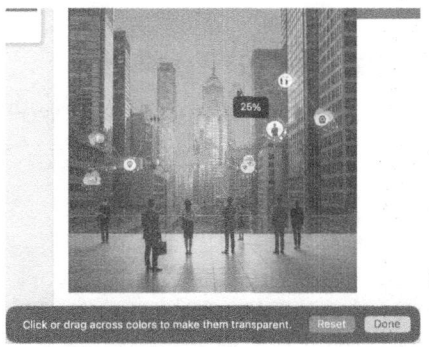

Before

After

Adding and Customizing Shapes

Duplicate the third slide and change the title to "Quarterly Objectives." Remove the image. To highlight key metrics, we'll add a shape to the this slide.

① Click on the **Shape** button in the toolbar and select a rectangle.

② Draw the rectangle at the bottom of the title.

③ With the shape selected, click on the **Style** tab in the **Format** sidebar. Customize the fill color, border, and shadow to match the presentation's theme.

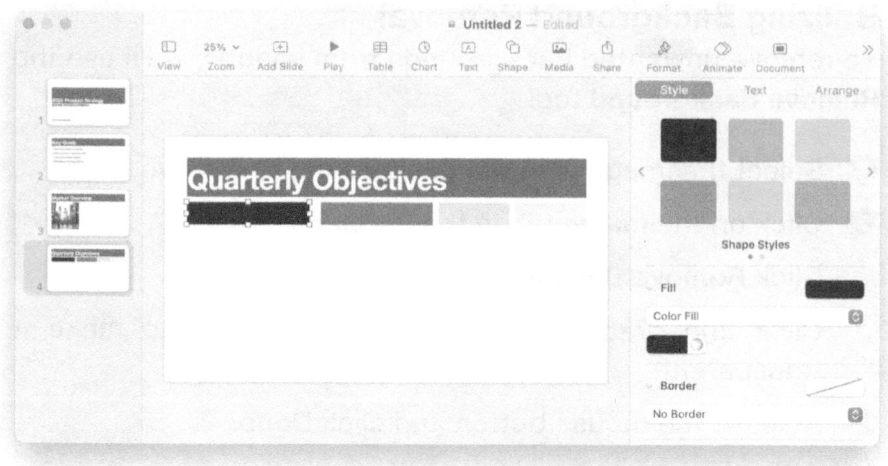

Combining Shapes for Custom Graphics

To create a unique graphic representing growth, we'll combine multiple shapes.

1. Insert a triangle and a rectangle onto the slide.

2. Position the triangle atop the rectangle to form an arrow.

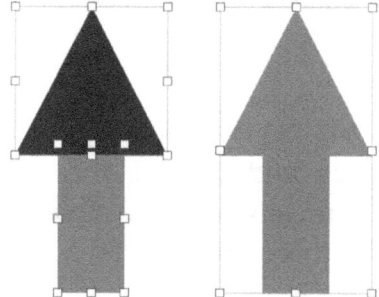

3. Select both shapes by holding the **Shift** key and clicking each.

4. Click on the **Format** menu, choose **Shapes and Lines**, then select **Unite**.

Combining shapes allows for the creation of custom graphics tailored to specific presentation needs.

Incorporating Icons

Duplicate the third slide and change the title to **"Team Structure**." To visually represent different departments, we'll add relevant icons to this slide.

1 Navigate to the **"Team Structure"** slide.

2 Click on the **Shape** button and browse on the shapes categories.

3 Insert icons representing departments like **Sales**, **Marketing**, and **Development**.

4 Resize and position the icons adjacent to their corresponding text labels.

Icons provide quick visual cues, enhancing comprehension and retention.

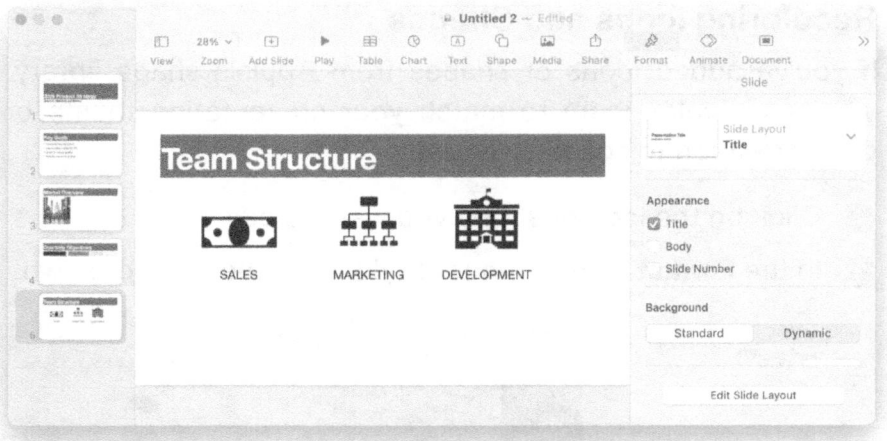

Aligning and Distributing Visual Elements

To maintain a clean layout, we'll align and distribute the icons evenly.

1 Select all the icons by holding the **Shift** key and clicking each.

2 Click on the **Arrange** tab in the **Format** sidebar.

③ Use the **Align** options to align the icons horizontally.

④ Use the **Distribute** options to evenly space the icons.

Proper alignment ensures a professional and organized appearance.

Recoloring Icons and Shapes

If you've added icons or shapes from Apple's shape library, you can recolor them to match your presentation theme or draw attention to specific visuals.

① Click on the icon or shape you want to edit.

② In the **Format** sidebar under **Style**, click the **Fill** dropdown.

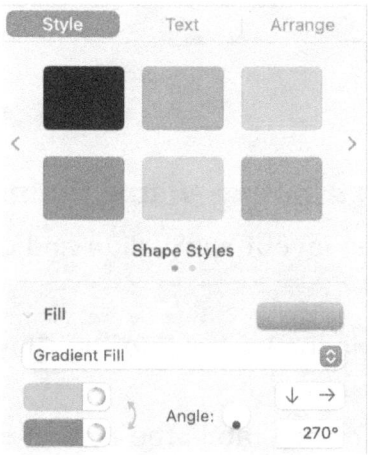

③ Choose a solid color, gradient, or even image fill. For consistent branding, match the color with your theme's accent color.

④ If using gradients, select the **Gradient Fill** and adjust the angle, color stops, and opacity.

Creating Callouts with Speech and Thought Bubbles

Shapes can also be used as expressive visual elements—like speech bubbles or callouts—to highlight comments or quotes.

① Click the **Shape** button in the toolbar.

② Scroll to the Callouts category and select a **Speech Bubble** or **Rounded Rectangle** with a pointer.

③ Place it near the part of the slide you want to annotate— such as near the market image on your **"Market Overview"** slide.

④ Double-click inside the bubble to add text like: **"Emerging Region Growth Focus."**

⑤ Format the bubble with a bold border and fill color using the **Style** tab.

Grouping and Locking Visual Elements

Once you've arranged a combination of images, shapes, and text that should stay together—such as a callout or label—it's helpful to group and lock them.

① Select all elements you want to group by **Shift-clicking** them.

② **Right-click** and choose **Group**, or use **Arrange > Group** from the top menu.

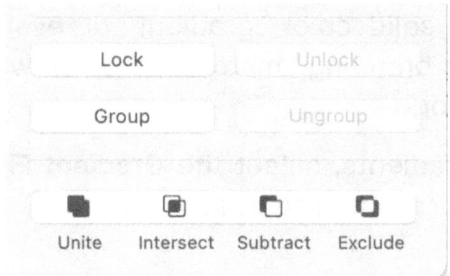

③ Once grouped, go to the **Arrange** tab and click **Lock**.

This ensures your callouts or icons remain in place even if you adjust other content on the slide.

Using Opacity for Layering Effects

Adjusting opacity is useful when layering shapes or placing text over images. You can soften backgrounds without losing visual context.

① Select the image or shape you want to adjust.

② In the **Style** section of the **Format** sidebar, use the **Opacity** slider.

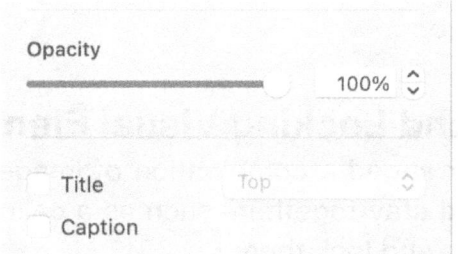

③ Set the value anywhere between 30–70% depending on how much fade you want.

For example, on the "2025 Product Strategy" title slide, you could add a semi-transparent white rectangle behind your title to boost contrast over a busy photo background.

Aligning Visuals Across Multiple Slides

To maintain a unified design, align key elements like logos, icons, or dividers consistently across slides.

1. Add a logo (or shape) to one slide.

2. Right-click and select **Copy**.

3. Navigate to each slide where the element should appear, then use **Paste** and manually place it using alignment guides.

4. Alternatively, add the element to the master slide layout if it's used everywhere.

Aligning visuals across slides helps tie your content together and makes transitions smoother.

USING TABLES AND CHARTS FOR DATA VISUALIZATION

Data tells a story. When presented clearly, it can inform, persuade, and inspire. Keynote provides intuitive tools to transform raw numbers into compelling visuals, allowing your audience to grasp complex information at a glance.

Continuing with our "2025 Product Strategy" presentation, we'll delve into creating and customizing tables and charts. From inserting data tables to designing interactive charts, each step will build upon the previous, ensuring a cohesive and informative presentation.

Inserting a Data Table

To present our quarterly objectives, we'll begin by adding a table to the "Quarterly Objectives" slide.

1. Navigate to the "**Quarterly Objectives**" slide.

2. Click on the **Table** button in the toolbar.

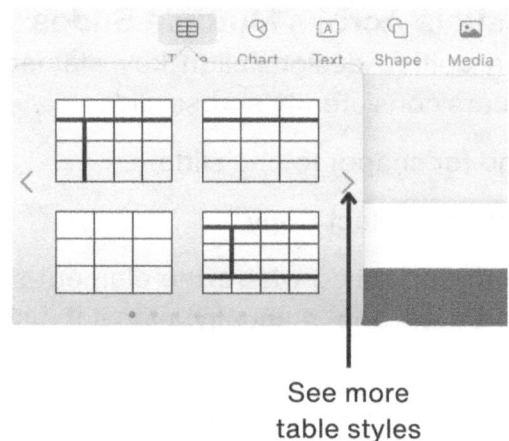

See more
table styles

③ Choose a table style that complements your presentation's theme.

④ Click to insert the table onto the slide.

⑤ Adjust the number of rows and columns as needed by clicking the **Add Row** or **Add Column** buttons.

This table will serve as the foundation for our data visualization, outlining key performance indicators for each quarter.

Populating the Table with Data

With the table in place, we'll input our quarterly objectives and corresponding targets.

① Click on the first cell and enter the header: **Objective**.

② Fill in the subsequent headers: **Q1, Q2, Q3, Q4**.

③ In the rows below, input objectives such as **Increase Market Share**, **Launch New Product**, **Improve Customer Satisfaction**, and **Expand to New Regions**.

④ Enter the target percentages or figures for each objective per quarter.

This structured layout provides a clear overview of our strategic goals throughout the year.

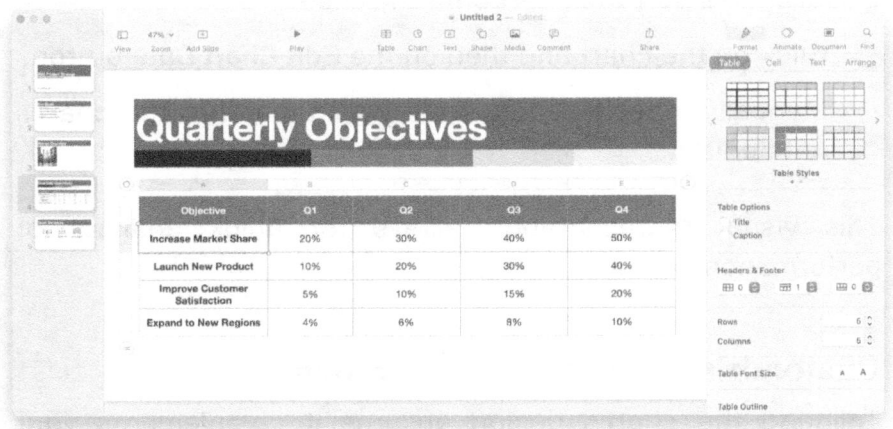

Formatting the Table for Clarity

A well-formatted table enhances readability and emphasizes key data points.

1. Select the entire table.

2. In the **Format** sidebar, click on the **Table** tab.

3. Choose a color scheme that aligns with your brand colors.

4. Adjust the text alignment and font size for optimal readability.

5. Apply bold formatting to header rows for distinction.

These adjustments ensure that your table is both visually appealing and easy to interpret.

Converting Table Data into a Chart

To visualize trends and comparisons, we'll transform our table data into a chart.

1. Click on the **Chart** button in the toolbar.

② Select a chart type suitable for your data, such as a **Line Chart** or **Bar Chart**.

③ Click to insert the chart onto the slide.

④ Click on the chart and then on the **Edit Chart Data** button.

⑤ Manually input the data from your table into the chart's data editor.

This visual representation allows for quick analysis of performance across quarters.

Customizing the Chart Appearance

Tailoring the chart's design ensures it complements your presentation's aesthetics.

① Select the chart to activate the **Format** sidebar.

② Under the **Chart** tab, choose a style that matches your theme.

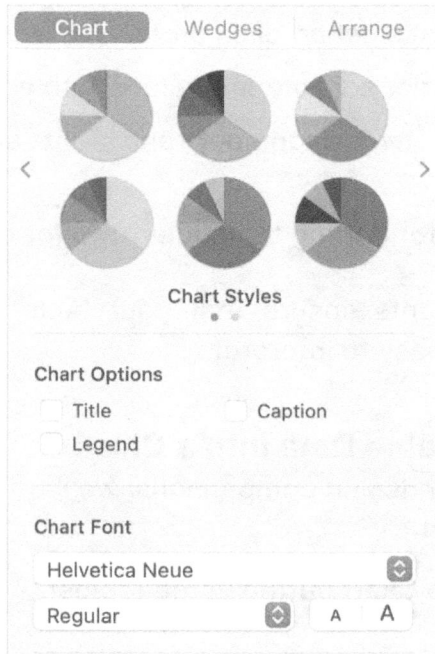

③ Adjust the colors of data series to differentiate between objectives.

④ Add data labels for precise values.

⑤ Include a chart title and legend for context.

A well-designed chart not only conveys information but also enhances audience engagement.

Creating Interactive Charts

Interactive charts allow viewers to explore data dynamically, revealing different data sets upon interaction.

① Insert an Interactive **Chart** by clicking on the **Chart** button and selecting the **Interactive** tab.

② Choose a chart type, such as **Column** or **Scatter**.

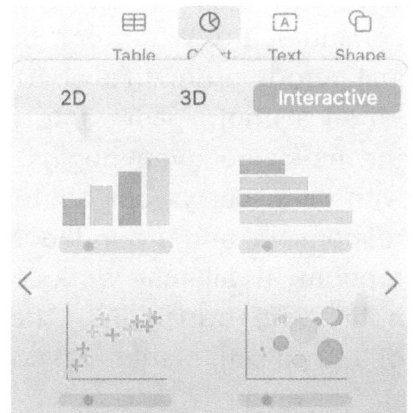

③ Input your data into the chart's data editor, assigning each data set to a different interaction point.

④ Customize the chart's appearance as previously described.

⑤ During the presentation, use the interactive controls to navigate through data sets.

This feature is particularly useful for comparing different scenarios or time periods.

CHAPTER 3

Animations and Transitions

A presentation moves at the pace you set. Every transition, every animation is a cue. It tells the audience what to look at, what to hold on to, and what's coming next. Done well, motion doesn't distract—it guides. It brings in energy, adds rhythm, and makes information easier to absorb without ever speaking a word. And with Keynote, movement is never just flash. It's precision. Controlled, intentional, and always part of the flow.

The motion on a slide isn't there to impress—it's there to communicate. When one bullet appears after another, it isn't just about order. It's about revealing an idea step-by-step. When a photo glides into place, it anchors attention before the message even begins. These small shifts, when added with care, carry your content forward in ways that feel fluid, responsive, and grounded. Nothing feels abrupt. Nothing feels random. It all just works. And when it does, people don't notice the transitions. They notice the message that was delivered with clarity and confidence.

ADDING SLIDE TRANSITIONS

Movement between slides should feel natural. Each transition is an opportunity to guide your audience's attention, setting the pace and tone for the information that follows. In Keynote, transitions are more than just visual effects—they're tools to enhance storytelling.

Continuing with our "2025 Product Strategy" presentation, we'll explore how to apply and customize slide transitions to create a cohesive and engaging flow. From subtle fades to dynamic movements, each transition will be tailored to support the narrative of our presentation.

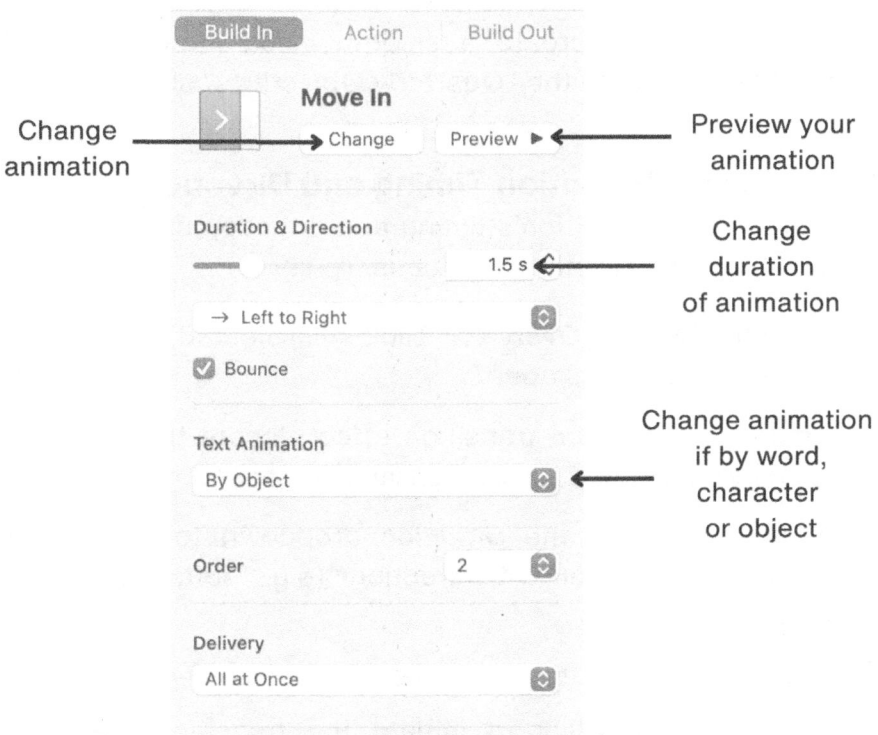

Applying a Basic Slide Transition

To begin, we'll add a simple transition between the "**Market Overview**" and "**Quarterly Objectives**" slides.

1 Open your **Keynote** presentation and navigate to the "**Market Overview**" slide.

2 In the slide navigator, select the "**Market Overview**" slide.

3 Click on the **Animate** button in the toolbar to open the animation sidebar.

4. In the **Transitions** section, click **Add an Effect**.

5. Choose a transition effect, such as **Magic Move**.

6. Adjust the transition settings, including duration and direction, as desired.

7. Click **Preview** to see the transition in action.

This transition will create a smooth visual flow from the "Market Overview" to the "Quarterly Objectives" slide.

Customizing Transition Timing and Direction

Fine-tuning the transition's timing and direction can enhance the presentation's rhythm and focus.

1. With the "**Market Overview**" slide still selected, ensure the Animate sidebar is open.

2. Under the selected transition effect, locate the **Duration** slider and adjust it to set the transition speed.

3. If available, use the **Direction** dropdown to select the transition's movement direction (e.g., left, right, up, down).

4. Decide when the transition should start:
   - Select **On Click** to initiate the transition manually during the presentation.
   - Select **Automatically** to have the transition occur after a set delay; adjust the **Delay** setting as needed.

Applying Transitions to Multiple Slides

To maintain consistency, you can apply the same transition effect to multiple slides simultaneously.

1. In the slide navigator, hold down the **Command** (⌘) key and click to select each slide you want to apply the transition to.

(2) With the slides selected, click on the **Animate** button in the toolbar.

(3) In the **Transitions** section, click **Add an Effect**.

(4) Choose your desired transition effect.

(5) Adjust the transition settings as needed.

Removing or Changing a Transition

If a transition no longer suits your presentation's flow, you can easily modify or remove it.

(1) Select the slide with the transition you want to change or remove.

(2) Click on the **Animate** button in the toolbar.

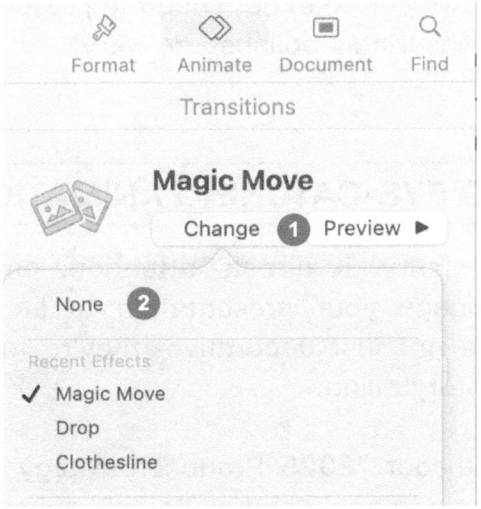

(3) In the Transitions section, click **Change (1)**.

(4) To select a different transition, choose a new effect from the list.

(5) To remove the transition entirely, select **None (2)**.

Previewing All Transitions in Sequence

Before presenting, it's beneficial to preview your slides to ensure transitions flow smoothly.

1   Click on the **Play** button in the toolbar to start the presentation from the current slide.

2   Advance through the slides using the arrow keys or by clicking to observe each transition.

3   Note any transitions that feel abrupt or out of place and adjust them as needed.

Previewing allows you to experience the presentation as your audience will, ensuring a polished delivery.

CREATING EYE-CATCHING ANIMATIONS

Motion adds clarity. It directs attention, emphasizes key points, and brings your presentation to life. In Keynote, animations are not just decorative—they're functional tools that enhance storytelling.

Continuing with our "2025 Product Strategy" presentation, we'll explore how to apply and customize animations to make our content more engaging. From introducing text elements to animating charts, each step will build upon the last, creating a cohesive and dynamic presentation.

Animating Text for Emphasis

To highlight our key goals, we'll animate the text to appear sequentially, maintaining audience engagement.

1 Navigate to the slide with your list of goals.

2 Select the text box containing the list.

3 Click on the **Animate** button in the toolbar to open the animation sidebar.

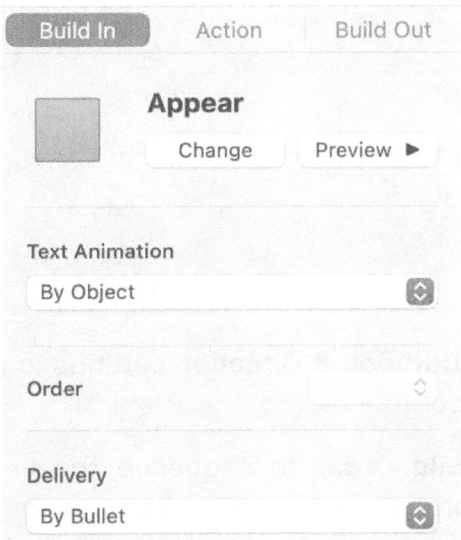

4 Under the **Build In** tab, click **Add an Effect** and choose **Appear** or another preferred effect.

5 In the **Delivery** dropdown, select **By Bullet** to animate each point individually.

Animating Images to Illustrate Points

Visuals can reinforce your message when introduced thoughtfully.

1 Insert the relevant image onto your slide.

2 Select the image and open the **Animate** sidebar.

3 Under the **Build In** tab, click **Add an Effect** and choose an effect like **Move In**.

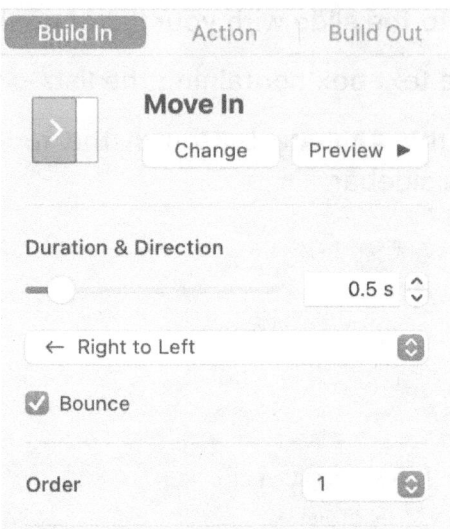

4 Adjust the **Duration & Direction** settings to match the flow of your presentation.

5 Use the **Build Order** to sequence the image animation after the corresponding text point.

This technique visually reinforces the information, making it more memorable for the audience.

Animating Charts to Reveal Data Gradually

Gradual revelation of chart data can help maintain audience focus and build anticipation.

1 Insert your chart onto the slide.

2 Select the chart and open the **Animate** sidebar.

3 Under the **Build In** tab, click **Add an Effect** and choose an appropriate animation, such as **Wipe** or **Dissolve**.

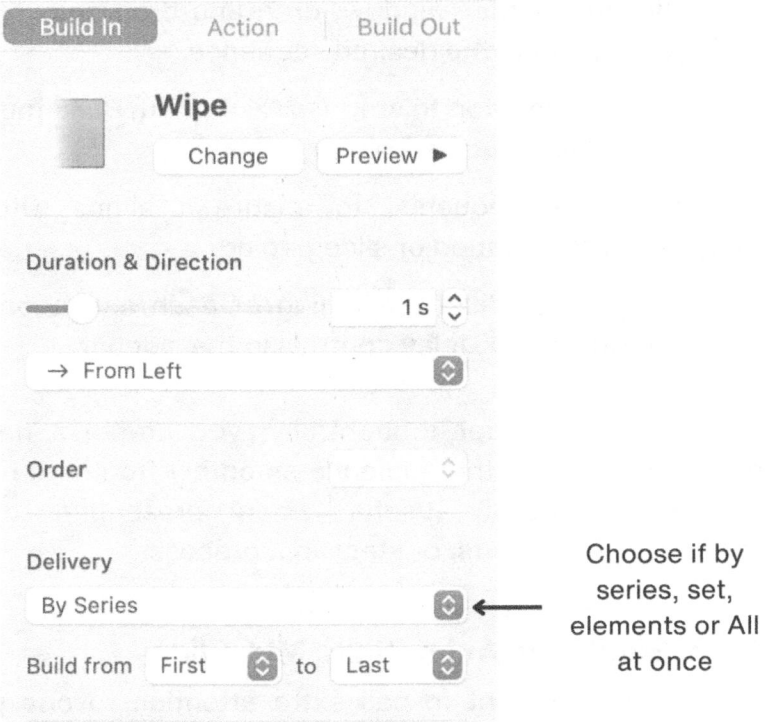

Choose if by series, set, elements or All at once

4 In the Delivery dropdown, select **By Series** or **By Element** in Series to control the data reveal sequence.

5 Adjust the **Duration** and **Delay** settings to pace the data introduction.

This method ensures the audience can digest complex data in manageable segments.

Sequencing Animations for Narrative Flow

Proper sequencing ensures your animations support the story you're telling.

1 After adding animations to your slide elements, click Build Order at the bottom of the Animate sidebar.

② In the **Build Order** window, drag and drop animations to arrange them in the desired sequence.

③ Set each animation to start **On Click**, **With Build [number]**, or **After Build [number]** to control timing.

④ Preview the sequence to ensure it aligns with your spoken presentation or slide pacing.

⑤ If necessary, adjust the timing of each animation using the **Duration** and **Delay** controls in the sidebar.

By using Build Order thoughtfully, you create a narrative rhythm that guides the audience smoothly from one point to the next—especially useful when presenting multiple objectives, data points, or steps in a process.

Using Emphasis Animations Mid-Slide

Sometimes you want to call extra attention to one part of your content while the rest stays in place. We'll use an emphasis animation to highlight a key goal: "Launch Q3 Software Updates."

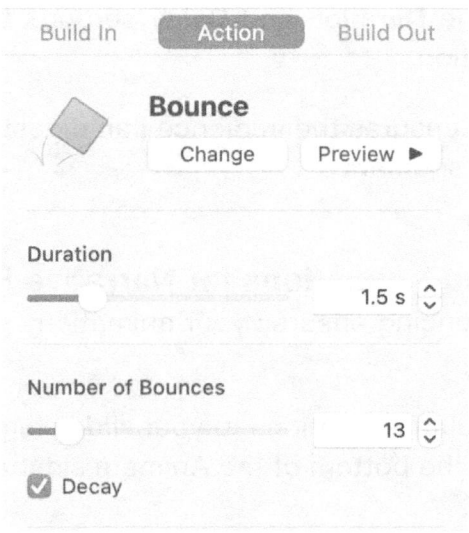

① On your slide listing quarterly goals, select the specific bullet or text box with **"Launch Q3 Software Updates."**

② In the **Animate** sidebar, open the **Action** tab and click **Add an Effect**.

③ Choose **Scale**, **Pulse**, or **Bounce** as your emphasis effect.

④ Adjust the **Duration** and **Repeat** settings for subtlety—don't overdo it.

⑤ Use **Build Order** to trigger the emphasis on click or immediately after a supporting point.

This animation adds motion without movement, making sure key details stand out clearly.

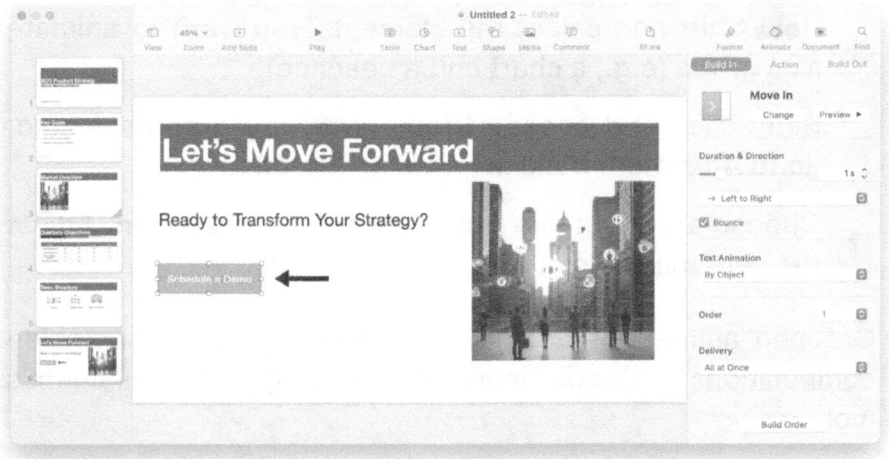

Call-to-Action Slide with Layered Animations

Toward the end of your presentation, we will create another slide. We'll build one now, using layered animations to create an engaging final call.

① Create a new slide titled **Let's Move Forward**.

② Add a central message in a large text box: **Ready to Transform Your Strategy?**

③ Insert a shape below it—such as a button-style rectangle—and add text: **Schedule a Demo**.

④ Animate the headline text using **Build In** > **Fade & Scale**.

⑤ Animate the button shape using **Build In** > **Move In** from the bottom.

⑥ Use **Build Order** to show the button **After Build 1**, with a slight delay.

Grouping Elements for Unified Animation

If you want to animate multiple elements together—such as a title and supporting graphic—you'll need to group them first.

① Hold Shift and select the elements you want to animate as a group (e.g., a chart and a headline).

② Right-click and choose **Group**. With the group selected, go to **Animate** > **Build In** > **Add an Effect**.

③ Choose an effect like **Scale**, **Dissolve**, or **Move In**. Adjust the settings as usual.

Grouped animations are great for bringing in complex slide compositions without manually syncing each element's motion.

USING MAGIC MOVE FOR SEAMLESS EFFECTS

Magic Move isn't just a transition—it's a subtle storytelling engine. With a single tap, Keynote lets you animate the movement, scale, and opacity of objects between two slides, creating fluid, cinematic transitions that feel like design magic. Duplicate a slide, shift elements where you want them to go—text blocks, images, shapes—and Keynote handles the animation in between. The result is motion that feels intentional, smooth, and elegant, like your presentation is thinking ahead for your audience.

What makes **Magic Move** powerful is how *invisible* it is. There are no timelines to manage, no keyframes to fiddle with. Want your chart to fly into place or your product photo to gently zoom across the screen? Just move it on the duplicate slide. Keynote's intelligent engine does the rest—animating changes with the same finesse you expect from Apple's design DNA. Whether you're pitching an idea or narrating a journey, Magic Move helps you glide from one point to the next, making your message not just seen, but felt.

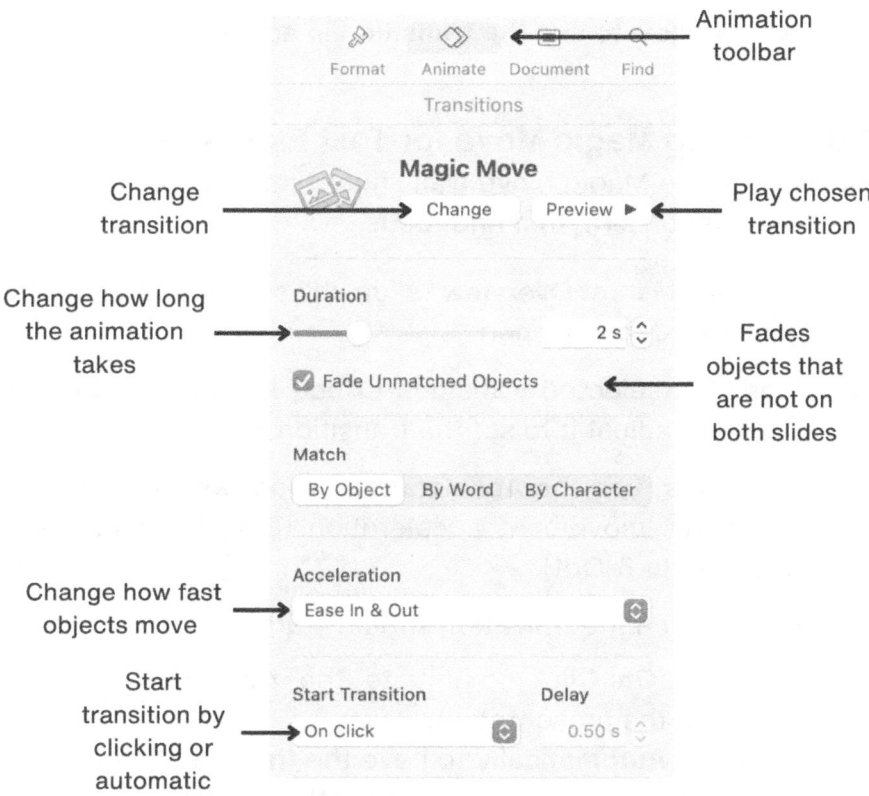

Applying a Basic Magic Move Transition

To begin, we'll add a simple Magic Move transition between the "**Market Overview**" and "**Quarterly Objectives**" slides.

1. Open your Keynote presentation and navigate to the "**Market Overview**" slide.

2. In the slide navigator, select the "**Market Overview**" slide.

3. Click on the **Animate** button in the toolbar to open the animation sidebar.

4. In the **Transitions** section, click **Add an Effect** and choose **Magic Move**.

5. Adjust the transition settings, including duration and acceleration, as desired.

6. Click **Preview** to see the transition in action,

Customizing Magic Move for Text Elements

Fine-tuning the Magic Move transition's settings can enhance the presentation's rhythm and focus.

1. With the "**Market Overview**" slide still selected, ensure the **Animate** sidebar is open.

2. Under the selected transition effect, locate the **Duration** slider and adjust it to set the transition speed.

3. If available, use the **Acceleration** dropdown to select the transition's movement acceleration (e.g., Ease In, Ease Out, Ease In & Out).

4. Decide when the transition should start:
   - Select **On Click** to initiate the transition manually during the presentation.
   - Select **Automatically** to have the transition occur after a set delay; adjust the **Delay** setting as needed.

CHAPTER 4

Advanced Keynote Features

Everything in a presentation happens on the surface—until it doesn't. Behind the slides, there's a deeper layer of features working quietly in the background. They save time. They sharpen collaboration. They unlock controls you wouldn't expect from something this simple. And while you may not see them when the deck plays, you feel their impact every time you work with someone else, fine-tune a delivery, or export your work in just the right format.

The experience isn't just about design anymore. It's about precision, automation, and flow—how quickly you can edit, respond, revise, and share. Tools that track your changes or let someone else drop a comment without sending a file back and forth. Tools that let you speak, and the words appear. Tools that turn a Keynote file into something else entirely. These features don't change what you say—they change how effortlessly you say it.

WORKING WITH LIVE VIDEO AND INTERACTIVE WIDGETS

Integrating live video and interactive elements into your Keynote presentation can elevate your content, making it more engaging and dynamic. These features allow you to present real-time demonstrations, interact with your audience, and create a more immersive experience.

Adding Live Video to a Slide

This feature is particularly useful for adding a personal touch to your presentation, allowing you to appear on-screen alongside your content.

1. Open your Keynote presentation and navigate to the slide where you want to add the live video.

2. Click the **Media** button in the toolbar, then select **Live Video**.

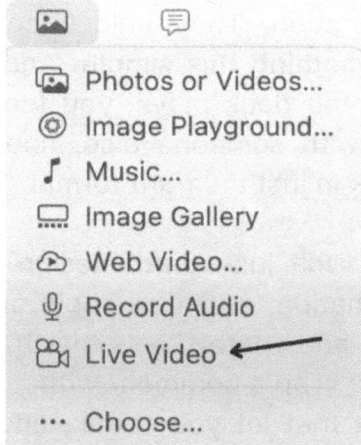

3. A live video window will appear on the slide, displaying the feed from your Mac's built-in camera.

4. To resize the live video window, drag the handles on the corners.

5. To reposition the live video window, click and drag it to the desired location on the slide.

Customizing Live Video Appearance

These customization options allow you to seamlessly integrate the live video into your slide's layout.

1 Select the live video window on your slide.

2 In the **Format** sidebar, click the b tab.

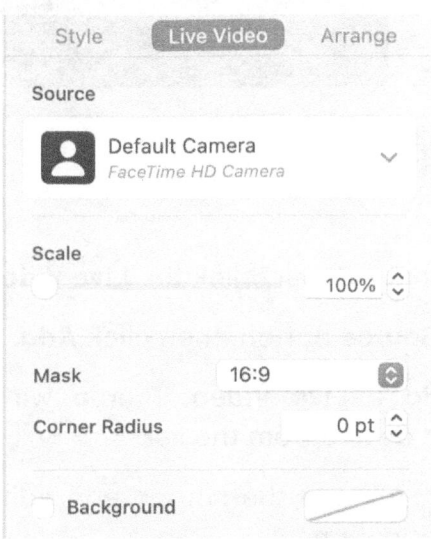

4 To adjust the corner radius, use the **Corner Radius** slider to make the corners more or less rounded.

5 To zoom in or out, use the **Scale** slider to adjust the size of the video feed within its frame.

Using External Cameras as Live Video Source

If you prefer to use an external camera or device as your live video source:

1 Connect your external camera, iPhone, or iPad to your Mac using a compatible cable.

2 In Keynote, select the live video window on your slide.

In the **Format** sidebar, click the **Live Video** tab.

Click the **Source** button, then click **Add**.

In the **Add a Live Video Source** window, select your connected device from the list.

Optionally, rename the source and edit its thumbnail for easy identification.

Click **Add** to include the new source in your presentation.

This setup is ideal for demonstrations, allowing you to showcase physical products or processes live during your presentation.

Managing Live Video During Presentations

To control the live video feed while presenting:

Start your slideshow by clicking **Play** in the toolbar.

To pause or resume the live video, move your cursor to reveal the presentation controls, then click the **Live Video** button to toggle the feed.

③ If you're using multiple live video sources, you can switch between them by clicking the **Source** button and selecting the desired feed.

These controls provide flexibility during your presentation, allowing you to manage live content seamlessly.

Adding Interactive Widgets with Linked Objects

Interactive widgets can enhance your presentation by allowing viewers to navigate through content non-linearly:

① Select the object (text box, shape, image) you want to use as an interactive element.

② Click the **Format** in the menu bar then select **Add Link**.

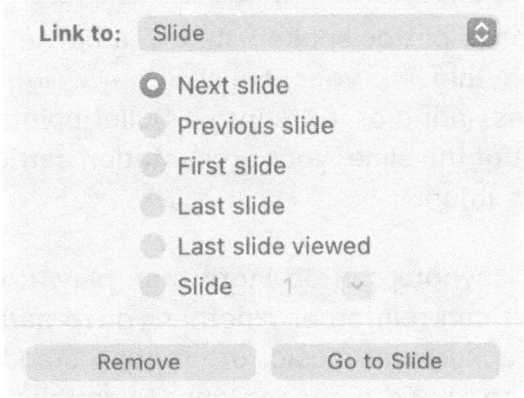

③ Choose **Slide** from the dropdown menu.

④ In the **Slide** menu, select the slide you want the object to link to.

This feature is useful for creating interactive menus, quizzes, or branching scenarios within your presentation.

Creating a Self-Guided Interactive Presentation

To design a presentation that viewers can navigate independently:

1. Set up your slides with interactive links as described above.

2. Go to **Document** in the toolbar, then click the **Presentation** tab.

3. Under **Presentation Type**, select **Self-Playing**.

4. Adjust the timing settings as needed, or set them to manual to allow viewers to control the pace.

ADDING VOICE NARRATION AND AUDIO ELEMENTS

Some content is better spoken than read. The tone in your voice, the rhythm of your pause, the weight of silence between slides—none of it fits into a bullet point. When voice becomes part of the slide, your presentation carries more than data. It carries intent.

Audio inside Keynote can do more than play. It can guide. It can explain. It can reinforce. Whether you're narrating slides, embedding background music, or creating standalone media decks, you don't need a second app. Everything you need is already built in.

Recording a Voiceover for the Entire Presentation

Use voice narration to guide viewers through your entire presentation. It's recorded slide by slide and plays automatically on export.

1. Open your Keynote presentation on Mac or iPad.

2. Click or tap **Play** > **Record Slideshow** from the toolbar.

③ When the interface appears, check your microphone level and click the red **Record** button.

④ Speak clearly as you walk through your presentation using arrow keys or gestures to advance slides.

⑤ To re-record any slide, go back and start recording from that point.

⑥ When finished, tap **Esc** or click **Stop Recording**.

⑦ To review your voiceover, play the presentation and listen for pacing, transitions, and clarity.

Adding Audio to a Single Slide

Some slides require their own sound—an effect, a voice, a short clip. Use slide-specific audio for focused control.

① On a slide, tap or click to select it.

② Go to **Media** > **Choose** from the toolbar.

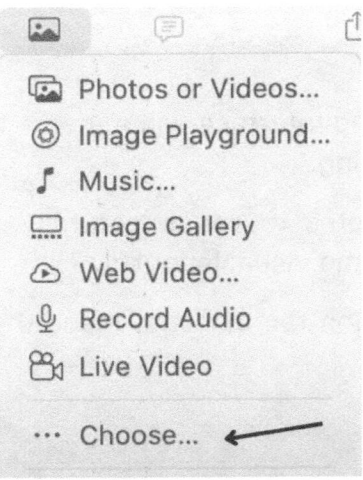

③ Browse your system and select the desired audio file.

④ The audio icon appears on the slide—position it off to the corner or hide it behind an image if needed.

⑤ Select the icon and open the **Format** panel.

⑥ Under **Audio**, select whether it plays **On Click**, **Automatically**, or **Loop**.

⑦ Click **Preview** to test playback directly in the editor.

Recording Audio Directly onto a Slide

Instead of importing a file, you can record your voice narration for individual slides right inside Keynote.

① On a slide, tap or click to select it.

② Tap or click the **Media** button, then choose **Record Audio**.

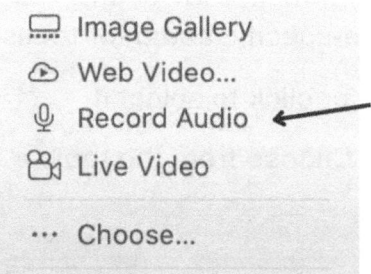

③ The recording interface will appear—tap the red button to begin speaking.

④ Use your notes to speak naturally, keeping the pacing matched to the visual layout.

⑤ Tap **Stop**, then tap Insert to place the new recording into the slide.

⑥ You'll see the small speaker icon on the canvas; reposition it if necessary.

⑦ You can play it back and re-record if needed from the same menu.

Trimming and Editing Audio Clips

Audio clips can be refined without leaving Keynote. Trim unwanted silence, align playback, or fade.

① Click or tap the audio icon on the slide.

② In the **Format > Audio** panel, tap **Edit Audio**.

③ Drag the start and end trim handles to crop the clip.

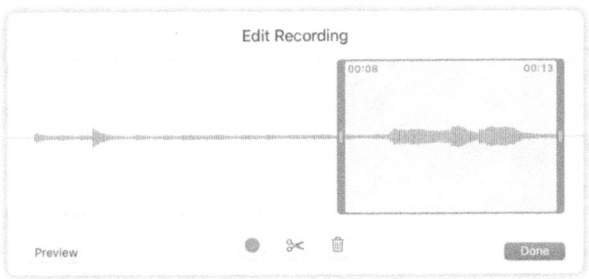

④ Use the playhead to find the exact section that needs cutting.

⑤ For cleaner transitions, tap **Fade In** or **Fade Out** and set duration.

⑥ Tap **Done** to save the clip edits in place.

Looping and Syncing Audio with Builds

Use looping audio for ambient effects or background music that matches animations.

① Select a slide in your presentation.

② Insert a soft music track using **Media > Music**.

③ Select the audio icon and go to **Format** > **Audio**.

④ Enable **Loop** and set playback to start **Automatically**.

⑤ Now, animate your slide using **Animate** > **Build In** for the content.

⑥ Open **Build Order** and align animations with your voiceover or music rhythm.

⑦ Use **Delay** between builds if needed to match the timing perfectly.

This creates a slide that animates naturally along with a background track, enhancing the flow.

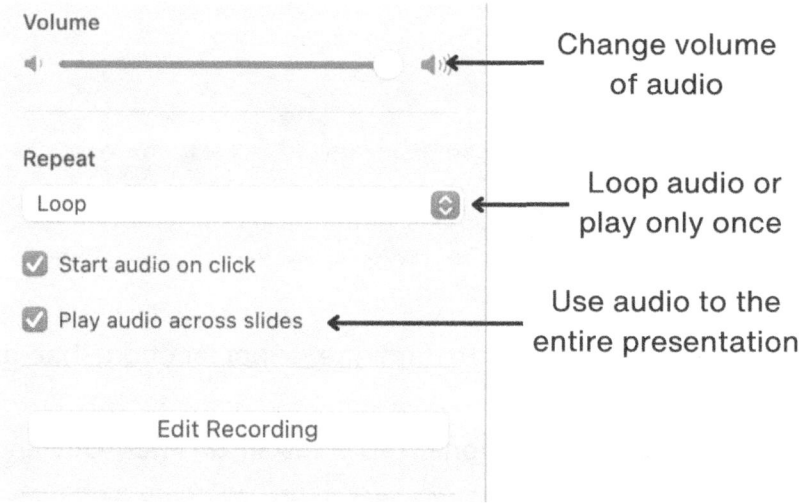

Adding Background Music to the Entire Presentation

For exported decks or self-guided playback, a soundtrack sets the tone across the entire deck.

① Click **Document** in the toolbar, then go to the **Audio** tab.

② Tap **+** to choose a file from your system—select a high-quality loopable track.

③ Check **Play Across Slides** and **Loop** if you want it to restart automatically.

④ Adjust the **Volume** so it doesn't overpower your voiceover.

⑤ Tap **Play** to test the full sequence with audio continuity between slides.

This is useful for kiosks, digital signage, or promotional decks with no live narration.

Using Multiple Audio Tracks in One Slide
Sometimes you'll want sound effects and voice narration to work together on the same slide.

① On your slide, insert your voiceover first using **Record Audio**.

② Then insert a sound effect (e.g., crowd cheer) using **Media > Audio**.

③ Position the two audio icons in the corner and label them for clarity.

④ Open **Build Order** from the **Animate** panel.

⑤ Set voice narration to play first, and the sound effect **After Build 1** or with a delay.

⑥ Adjust individual volumes under **Format > Audio**.

This layering adds texture and impact without sacrificing timing or clarity.

Controlling Audio During Playback

In presenter mode, you can manage audio live as you speak or guide a session.

- Start your presentation by tapping Play.

- Tap the screen lightly with your finger to reveal controls.

- If your slide contains audio, a Pause and Play option appears in the toolbar.

- Use this to mute background music or replay narration if requested.

- If you're using a Bluetooth keyboard, arrow keys work for advancing while audio plays.

INTEGRATING WITH APPLE PENCIL (IPAD USERS)

The way you build slides changes when you hold a pencil instead of tapping a screen. You can draw, mark, move, and write—all without ever switching tools. It's tactile, immediate, and designed to work without needing to think about how. Everything flows from the Pencil into your presentation in real time.

There's no separation between planning and presenting anymore. You can sketch a flowchart and animate it. You can circle a chart live while delivering your pitch. You can write your edits by hand, turn them into text, and publish your deck in one sitting. Keynote doesn't treat the Apple Pencil as an accessory—it treats it as a primary tool.

Drawing Directly on Slides

Use drawing tools to create handwritten notes, underline headings, sketch diagrams, or illustrate key points. Drawings remain editable and can be resized or animated later.

1. Open your presentation on iPad and navigate to a slide.

2. Tap the slide with your **Apple Pencil t**o automatically activate drawing mode.

3. Select a drawing tool from the bottom toolbar: **Pen**, **Marker**, **Pencil**, or **Crayon**.

4. Use the color palette to choose your ink color, or tap the color wheel to define a custom shade.

5. Adjust the stroke size by tapping your selected tool again and using the slider.

6. Begin drawing your timeline path, adding arrowheads, dates, or annotations freehand.

7. Tap **Done** in the top right when you're finished sketching.

Editing and Moving Drawings

You can make adjustments to your sketches without redrawing them completely.

1. Tap any drawing you've added to enter selection mode.

2. Tap **Edit Drawing** in the pop-up toolbar to reopen the drawing canvas.

3. Use the **Selection Tool** (lasso icon) to circle a portion of your drawing.

4. Drag the selected portion to a new location or tap **Delete** to remove it.

5. Use the resize handles to adjust overall size or rotate as needed. Tap **Done** to exit edit mode.

Using Scribble to Add Text

Apple Pencil with Scribble allows you to write anywhere and convert handwriting into typed text automatically.

① Tap a blank area on your slide using your **Apple Pencil**.

② A text box will appear—start writing directly into the box.

③ **Scribble** converts your handwriting into typed text on the fly.

④ Scratch out a word to delete it or draw a vertical line to insert space.

⑤ To format the text, tap it with your finger and use the formatting controls from the toolbar.

This is especially helpful for writing content fluidly without switching keyboards.

Annotating Slides During Playback

Real-time drawing during a live presentation adds spontaneity and clarity to explanations.

① Tap **Play** to begin presenting from the current slide.

② Swipe with your Apple Pencil to activate live annotation mode.

③ Use the toolbar to select a color or tool before marking up the slide.

④ Draw directly over content—underlines, arrows, circles, or callouts.

⑤ When finished, tap the screen once with your finger to exit annotation mode.

⑥ After your presentation ends, choose whether to **Keep Annotations** or **Discard**.

Live annotation is great for responding to audience questions or highlighting dynamic parts of a demo.

Navigating and Selecting with Pencil

Instead of tapping with your finger, Apple Pencil can be used to scroll, select, and move content depending on your preferred setup.

1. Go to **Settings** > **Apple Pencil** on your iPad.

2. Under **Pencil Behavior**, choose **Select and Scroll**.

3. Return to Keynote. Now you can use your Apple Pencil to tap objects, scroll through slide thumbnails, or select multiple items using the lasso tool.

This replaces finger interaction for creators who prefer to do all layout and design work with Pencil alone.

Using Hover (Apple Pencil 2nd Gen + M2 iPad)

If you're using an iPad that supports hover, you can preview interactions without touching the screen.

1. Hover the Pencil tip above the drawing toolbar to preview tools without activating them.

2. Hover over shapes or elements on the slide to preview their outlines before selecting.

3. Use hover to precisely align objects by hovering near alignment guides.

Hover preview improves precision when rearranging slide components or selecting drawing tools quickly.

CHAPTER 5

Presenting and Sharing Like a Pro

Nothing changes when the slides go full screen—except everything. Every gesture counts. Every second between transitions feels longer. And every word feels more deliberate because now you're not just building a presentation. You're delivering one. This is where the tools that helped you build it quietly shift into tools that help you perform it.

Presenting well isn't about adding more. It's about removing friction. The distractions disappear. The controls stay tucked where you need them. Transitions flow naturally, animations hit on cue, and you have room to focus on speaking, not managing. And once it's done, the same presentation transforms again—from something delivered live to something that can be shared, exported, published, or rewatched. When it's built right, presenting becomes second nature. And sharing doesn't mean simplifying—it means scaling, without changing what makes it work.

USING PRESENTER MODE AND REMOTE CONTROL

When you're ready to deliver your presentation, Keynote offers powerful tools to enhance your delivery and control. Presenter Mode provides a dedicated interface to keep you on track, while remote control options allow for seamless navigation, even when you're away from your primary device.

Presenter Display Options

Keynote's Presenter Display offers a customizable interface to assist during your presentation.

1. Connect your Mac to an external display, projector, or Apple TV.

2. In Keynote, choose **Play > Customize Presenter Display**.

3. Select the elements you want to display: current slide, next slide, presenter notes, timer, or clock.

4. Arrange these elements to suit your preferences.

5. To start the presentation, choose **Play > Play Slideshow**.

Presenting in a Window

For virtual presentations or multitasking, presenting in a window keeps your slides accessible alongside other applications.

1. Open your presentation in Keynote on Mac.

2. Choose **Play > Play Slideshow** in Window.

3. Resize and position the window as needed.

4. Use the presenter display window to view notes and upcoming slides.

This mode is ideal for video conferences, allowing you to manage your presentation and communication tools simultaneously.

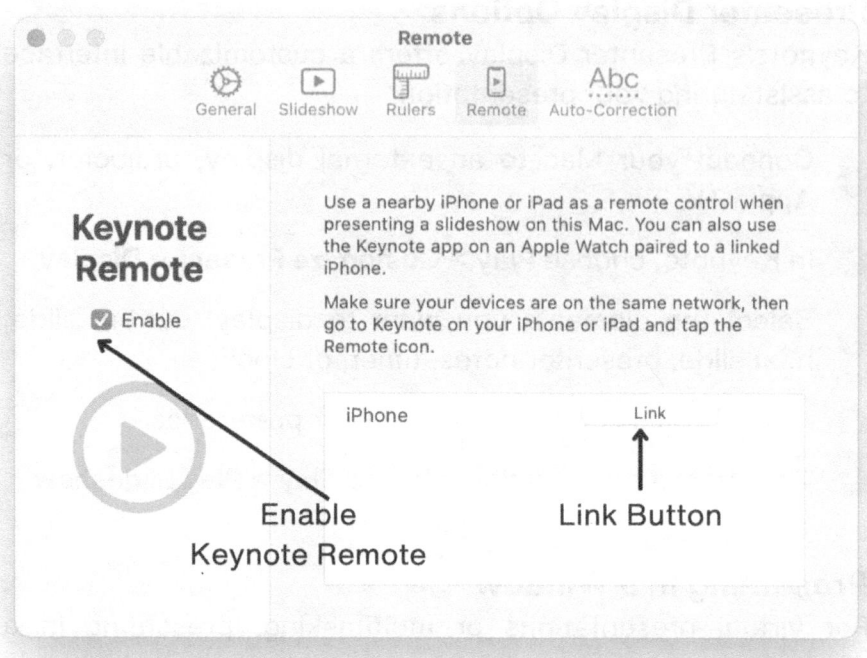

Enable
Keynote Remote

Link Button

Using Keynote Remote on iPhone or iPad

Control your presentation remotely using another Apple device.

1. Ensure both devices have Keynote installed and are on the same Wi-Fi network.

2. On your Mac, open Keynote and go to **Keynote** > **Settings** > **Remotes**, then enable **Allow Remote Control**.

3. On your iPhone or iPad, open Keynote and tap the **Remote** button.

4. Select your Mac from the list and enter the four-digit code displayed.

5. Once connected, use your device to navigate slides, view presenter notes, and even annotate slides in real-time.

This feature provides flexibility, allowing you to move freely while maintaining control over your presentation.

Using Apple Watch as a Remote

For hands-free control, your Apple Watch can serve as a convenient remote.

1 Ensure your iPhone is set up as a **Keynote Remote** and paired with your Apple Watch.

2 Open the Keynote app on your **Apple Watch**.

3 Start your presentation on your Mac or iPad.

4 Use your Apple Watch to advance slides, go back, or view the current slide.

EXPORTING AND SHARING (PDF, POWERPOINT, VIDEO

Once your presentation is complete, Keynote offers multiple export options to share your work across various platforms and formats. Whether you need a static document, a compatible file for collaboration, or a dynamic video, Keynote provides the tools to deliver your content effectively.

Format	Best For	Steps	Special Options
PDF	Creating static handouts or archives	1. **File → Export To → PDF** 2. Choose slide range and options (e.g., presenter notes) 3. Click **Next → Name file → Select destination** 4. Click **Export**	Preserves slide layout for printing or sharing
PowerPoint (.pptx)	Collaborating with PowerPoint users	1. **File → Export To → PowerPoint** 2. Review export options 3. Click **Next → Name file → Select destination → Export**	Fully compatible with Microsoft PowerPoint

Video (.mov)	Sharing on video platforms or asynchron ous delivery	1. **File → Export To → Movie** 2. Set slide duration, resolution, and playback options 3. Click **Next → Name file → Select destination → Export**	Ideal for uploading to YouTube or sending pre-recorded presentations

Sharing via iCloud

To collaborate in real-time:

1. Open your Keynote presentation.

2. Click the **Collaborate** button in the toolbar.

3. Choose the sharing method (e.g., Mail, Messages, Copy Link).

4. Set permissions for who can access and edit the presentation.

5. Send the invitation to collaborators.

This enables seamless collaboration across Apple devices.

LIVE STREAMING AND ONLINE PRESENTATIONS

Delivering presentations remotely requires tools that maintain clarity, engagement, and control. Keynote offers features that integrate seamlessly with live streaming platforms, ensuring your message is conveyed effectively, regardless of your audience's location.

Presenting in a Window

For virtual presentations, presenting in a window allows you to manage your slides alongside other applications.

1. Open your Keynote presentation on Mac.

2. Choose **Play** > **Play Slideshow** in Window.

75

③ Resize and position the window as needed.

④ Use the presenter display window to view notes and upcoming slides.

This setup is ideal for video conferences, allowing you to manage your presentation and communication tools simultaneously.

Sharing Your Screen

To broadcast your presentation during a live stream or video call:

① Start your video conferencing application (e.g., Zoom, Microsoft Teams).

② Begin your Keynote presentation in windowed mode.

③ In your conferencing app, select the Keynote window as the screen to share.

④ Ensure your microphone and camera are active for audience interaction.

Using Presenter Display

Maintain access to your notes and upcoming slides without displaying them to your audience.

① Connect your Mac to an external display or use virtual desktops.

② In Keynote, choose **Play** > **Customize Presenter Display**.

③ Select the elements you want to display: current slide, next slide, presenter notes, timer, or clock.

④ Arrange these elements to suit your preferences.

This setup ensures you have all necessary information at a glance without displaying it to your audience.

Recording for On-Demand Viewing

Create a recorded version of your presentation for audiences to view at their convenience.

1. Open your Keynote presentation.

2. Go to **File** > **Export To** > **Movie**.

3. Set the desired playback settings, including slide duration and resolution.

4. Click **Next**, then choose the destination and file name.

5. Click **Export** to generate the video file.

Share the exported video through your preferred platform or embed it on your website for on-demand access.

Engaging Your Remote Audience

Enhance interaction and maintain engagement during your live presentation.

- Use annotations to highlight key points in real-time.
- Incorporate polls or Q&A sessions through your conferencing platform.
- Encourage audience participation by prompting discussions or feedback.

These strategies help create a dynamic and interactive experience for your remote audience.

CONCLUSION

There's no difference between the keynote on stage and the one in your hand—except maybe where the applause comes from. When the tools are designed right, you don't have to think about the interface. You think about what you're saying, what you're showing, what you're trying to make land. Everything else—the transitions, the layouts, the formats, the playback—just works around you, quietly and instantly.

That's what Keynote offers. Not more buttons or features for the sake of having them. Just the ones that matter, exactly where you need them, exactly when you do. You can build it on the fly, or prepare every second down to the frame. You can draw, speak, layer, animate, export, stream—without losing time toggling tools or rethinking your structure. And whether you're at a desk, on a call, or standing in front of a crowd, the presentation is always just as polished as you are. When the details disappear, what you're left with is focus. And what your audience sees is clarity.

KEYNOTE TIPS FOR STUNNING PRESENTATIONS

Keynote is designed to make presentations effortless, beautiful, and precise. But if you only use the basics, you're missing out on the details that give your deck that refined Apple polish. Here are 7 unique, advanced tips that aren't commonly shared—but once you know them, they'll change how you build and deliver in Keynote.

Use SF Pro and SF Symbols for a Native Apple Look

Want your deck to look like something straight out of Cupertino? Use **SF Pro**, Apple's system font. It's not in the default Keynote font list, but you can download it at https://developer.apple.com/fonts/ . Once installed, it works system-wide. Pair it with SF Symbols—Apple's icon set—by downloading the **SF Symbols** app. You can drag icons into Keynote, convert them to vector outlines using **Format > Shapes > Make Editable**, and recolor them to match your palette.

Recolor Any Image with Tint

Want all your icons or graphics to match your theme color, even if they came in black, blue, or gray? Select the image, go to **Format > Image > Style**, and use **Color Overlay**. Choose any color, set the blend mode to **Multiply** or **Overlay**, and adjust the opacity. This trick works best on SVGs or PNGs with transparency. It creates a unified look across slides, especially for logos or app screenshots.

Turn Shapes Into Animated Masks

Here's something most presenters miss: you can animate **image reveals through shapes**. Insert an image, then draw a shape over it. Select both, go to **Format > Image > Mask with Shape**. Now animate that shape using **Move In** or **Scale** under the **Build In** tab. The image will animate with the shape, giving you cinematic reveals or zoom-ins without needing video editing software.

Create Smooth Parallax Slides with Background Layers

To add depth and movement, use **parallax effects** between slides. Duplicate your slide, then on the second version, move foreground elements (text, icons) slightly to the left or right, while shifting background elements (photos, shapes) in the opposite direction. Apply **Magic Move** as the transition. The subtle differential motion creates a clean parallax illusion— perfect for emphasizing change or narrative flow.

Add Video as a Texture

Forget flat backgrounds. You can use short looping videos as a texture behind content. Insert a full-screen video (MP4 or MOV), then reduce opacity or place a semi-transparent rectangle over it to soften. Use muted, abstract clips—like fog, water, or city lights—for motion without distraction. Set **Format > Movie > Start Movie on Click: OFF** and **Repeat: LOOP** to keep it running continuously.

Control Slide Movement with Keyboard Shortcuts Only

When you present, you don't have to use a clicker or mouse. Use **keyboard shortcuts** to stay fully focused. Press **X** during a slideshow to **turn the screen black**, **W** to **turn it white**, or **H** to **hide/show the pointer. Press** ⌘ + **Option** + **P** to toggle presenter display, and arrow keys to jump between builds instead of whole slides. It's fast, quiet, and keeps your delivery seamless.

Link Objects to Slides for Nonlinear Navigation

Keynote isn't just for linear storytelling. You can turn it into an **interactive deck**, like a guided app demo or product menu. Select any shape or text, then go to **Format > Add Link > Slide** and choose the target slide. Now clicking that object jumps the viewer to another part of the deck. Combine with invisible buttons for a clean look. It's perfect for live demos, product walk-throughs, or interactive kiosks.

AVOIDING COMMON PRESENTATION MISTAKES

Not every mistake breaks a presentation. But the wrong one, at the wrong time, can shift attention away from your content. Sometimes it's a pacing issue. Sometimes it's the moment you try to click and nothing happens. Most of the time, it's preventable. Not with extra features—but with better habits and clear steps.

Using Too Many Transitions

Transitions are helpful for pacing, but overusing them can distract your audience. Stick to one or two transition styles per deck. Use Dissolve, Fade, or Move In for subtle flow. Avoid novelty transitions unless they serve a visual cue.

Embedding Unsupported Media Files

Some video and audio formats won't play on all devices or export correctly. Use media encoded as .mp4 for video and .m4a or .aac for audio. Always preview playback on the device you plan to present from. Export test slides before final delivery.

Animating Everything

If every word or object enters with movement, your audience tunes out quickly. Use Build In animations only when they emphasize a point or reveal complex ideas gradually. Don't animate static labels or decorative icons unless necessary. Balance clarity with movement.

Not Testing Presenter Notes in Playback

Presenter Notes may be perfectly written but useless if not visible where you need them. Connect to your external display early. Go to **Play** > **Customize Presenter Display** and confirm that **Presenter Notes** are enabled. Arrange slide previews and clocks before the event.

Made in United States
Cleveland, OH
10 November 2025

25643581R00049